Motive power recognition:1
LOCOMOTIVES

Colin J. Marsden

LONDON

IAN ALLAN LTD

First published 1981
This Edition 1984

ISBN 0 7110 1365 9

Published by Ian Allan Ltd, Shepperton, Surrey;
and printed by Ian Allan Printing Ltd at their works
at Coombelands in Runnymede, England.

Front cover, top:
*Tinsley depot in June 1982 with Classes
56, 37, 31 and 45 on show.* L. A. Nixon

Front cover, bottom:
Side elevation of Class 58 locomotive.

Introduction

From the introduction during the late 1950s of large numbers of diesel and electric classes, recognition of the different types, sub-classes, fixtures and fittings has always aroused much interest from young and old alike. This book, *Motive Power Recognition:1 Locomotives*, has been prepared to give the reader information and pictorial illustration of BR classes of diesel, electric, electro-diesel and steam in traffic during 1984, including a technical description as well as many of the detail differences that exist.

Now, during the 1980s, recognition of various sub classes is far easier than during the 1960s and 1970s, this is due to the British Railways five figure computer numbering system, adopted during the mid-1970s which indicates far more than just a locomotive number. The first two numbers of the five figure system indicates the locomotive class, usually the lower the number the lower powered the locomotive. Class numbers ranging between 01 and 60 are for diesel locomotives, 70 and 79 for DC electric or electro-diesel locomotives and between 80 and 89 for AC electric locomotives. 97 indicates Departmental and service locomotives, and 98 BR owned steam locomotives. The third digit will be the sub class number, giving railway operating staff information about the fittings of the particular locomotive, ie: what kind of heating fitted, or whether the locomotive is fitted for push-pull operation etc. Where no sub classes exist the locomotive numbering commences with this third digit. The last two figures are the locomotive running numbers.

Many detail differences such as make of boiler, brake equipment or electrical equipment exist within some classes, but cannot be recognised from the external appearance, their detail differences usually have a large bearing on the use of particular locomotives.

The current standard livery of the BR locomotive fleet is black below buffer beam level, yellow ends, blue body side and roof. Running numbers are applied one set on each side, usually on the driver's corner, under the cab window or directly behind the cab door, under the number should be the data panel and shed allocation stickers. The BR double arrow logo is normally applied to the centre of the body but on some classes it can be found under the driver's assistant's side window.

During the early 1980s various members of Classes 47, 56 and 86, and all members of Classes 50 and 58 emerged in revised or rail freight livery including wrap round yellow ends, large BR loco and number.

This book includes all general technical data and illustrations of Classes 01 to 98 and IC125 power cars. In no way can it possibly give all detail differences as with some classes each member is recognisable by some means or another, but it tries to give the majority of detail differences that can be immediately recognised when looking at a locomotive.

In this, the second edition of *Motive Power Recognition: 1 Locomotives*, we have been able to include line drawings which it is hoped will assist readers further in recognition of the classes and the identification of some of the component parts. Due to space restrictions only one side elevation of each type can be included, and reference to the illustrations will be required to locate components on the other side.

I would like to take this opportunity to thank Mr Graham Fenn for the preparation of the line drawings in this volume, BR/BREL staff at a number of locations for their valued assistance, and numerous photographers who have assisted in locating some of the rarer types.

The Editor of this volume would like to be notified of any major detail differences that have been omitted from this book by sending them, together with a photograph if possible to: The Editor, Motive Power Recognition, Ian Allan Ltd, Terminal House, Shepperton TW17 8AS.

Colin J. Marsden

Left:
The once sizeable fleet of Class 25 locomotives is now rapidly diminishing with large inroads being made to firstly vacuum braked, and more recently dual braked examples. Class 25/2 No 25.229 approaches Ulverston with a trip oil train from Carnforth on 10 February 1983. The nose end communicating doors on this example have been sealed up. Colin J. Marsden

Locomotive Types and Classifications

Class	Type	Detail Difference	Region of Allocation
03	0-6-0		Midland/Eastern/Western
08	0-6-0		All Regions
09	0-6-0		Southern
13	0-6-0 + 0-6-0		Eastern
20	Bo-Bo		Midland/Eastern/Scottish
25/1	Bo-Bo	Series 1 equipment	Midland
25/2	Bo-Bo	Series 2 equipment	Midland
25/3	Bo-Bo	Series 3 equipment	Midland
26/0	Bo-Bo	Basic locomotive	Scottish
26/1	Bo-Bo	Equipment differences	Scottish
27	Bo-Bo		Scottish
31/1	A1A-A1A	Basic locomotive	Midland/Eastern/Western
31/4	A1A-A1A	Dual/electric heat fitted	Eastern
33/0	Bo-Bo	Basic locomotive	Southern
33/1	Bo-Bo	Push-pull modified loco	Southern
33/2	Bo-Bo	Slim line profile loco	Southern
37	Co-Co		Eastern/Western/Scottish
40	1Co-Co1		Midland/Eastern
45/0	1Co-Co1	Steam heat fitted	Midland/Eastern
45/1	1Co-Co1	Electric heat fitted	Midland
46	1Co-Co1		Eastern
47/0	Co-Co	Basic locomotive	Midland/Eastern/Western/Scottish
47/3	Co-Co	No heat fitted	Midland/Eastern/Western
47/4	Co-Co	Electric/dual heat fitted	Midland/Eastern/Western/Scottish
47/7	Co-Co	Push-pull fitted	Scottish
47/9	Co-Co	Evaluation locomotive	Western
50	Co-Co		Western
56	Co-Co		Midland/Eastern/Western
58	Co-Co		Midland
253	Bo-Bo		Eastern/Western
254	Bo-Bo		Eastern/Scottish
73/0	Bo-Bo	Original design	Southern
73/1	Bo-Bo	Modified design	Southern
81	Bo-Bo		Scottish
82	Bo-Bo		Midland
83	Bo-Bo		Midland
85	Bo-Bo		Midland
86/0	Bo-Bo	Standard 80mph locomotive	Midland
86/1	Bo-Bo	Experimental 100mph loco	Midland
86/2	Bo-Bo	Standard 100mph locomotive	Midland
86/3	Bo-Bo	SAB wheel fitted loco	Midland
87/0	Bo-Bo	Standard locomotive	Midland
87/1	Bo-Bo	Thyristor control fitted loco	Midland
97	—	Departmental locomotive	—
98	2-6-2T	Vale of Rheidol steam loco	Midland

Above:
The fleets of Sulzer 12LDA-28B powered locomotives of Classes 45/0 and 45/1 are seen today operating regularly on London Midland, Eastern and Western regions, and make infrequent visits to both Southern and Scottish regions. Although to many enthusiasts the 'Peak' locomotives are of a basically ugly appearance with a total of 16 wheels, since their concept during the modernisation plans in the mid-1950s they have provided BR with one of the most reliable medium powered mixed traffic locomotives. No 45.051 departs from Bristol Bath Road depot on 2 June 1981. Colin J. Marsden

Below left:
Each locomotive operating on the BR system which is in capital stock, carries a five figured identification number. The first two digits indicate the locomotive class, the third the sub-class, and the fourth and fifth the individual locomotive reporting number, ie: No 45.110 is a Class 45 sub-section 1, and is the tenth of the fleet. In addition to a running number each locomotive carries an information panel giving the class and sub-class of the locomotive, the weight, brake force in tons, ETH (electric train heat), index number (if fitted), RA (route availability) number, and maximum permitted speed. These panels are normally in the running number area. Colin J. Marsden

Below right:
Each locomotive carries the BR double arrow logo. This is either applied to each corner under the cab windows, at one end (under the driver's assistant's window) or centrally on the body side (with the exception of locomotives in revised or Railfreight livery). During recent years an increasing number of locomotives, and now IC125 power cars, have been given names. All names applied since 1975 have been of the corporate identical style, however some older style plates are still in existence. The positioning of nameplates is not consistent but, if possible, are fixed in the centre of the locomotive's body just above mid-height. The BR logo and corporate style Western Mail *nameplate are shown here both in a mid-body position.* Colin J. Marsden

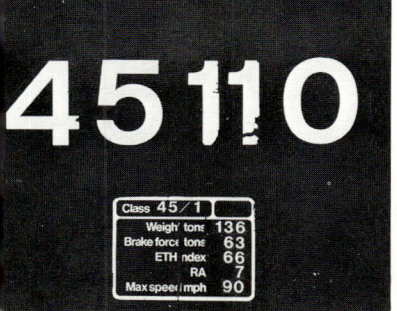

Class 03

Number series: 03.001-03.199, 03.370-03.399
Former number: D2000-D2199, D2370-D2399
Built by: BR
Introduced: From 1957
Type: 0-6-0
Weight in running order: 30.3 tonnes
Height: 11ft 9$\frac{3}{8}$in (3.59m)
Width: 8ft 6in (2.59m)
Length: 26ft 0in (7.92m)
Min curve negotiable: 2 chains (40.23m)
Max speed: 28$\frac{1}{2}$mph (42km/h)
Wheelbase: 9ft 0in (2.74m)
Wheel diameter: 3ft 7in (1.09m)
Brake type: Air, vacuum or dual
Sanding equipment: Pneumatic
Route availability: 1
Coupling restriction: *
Brake force: 13 tonnes
Engine type: Gardner 8L3
HP: 204hp (151kW)
Tractive effort: 15,300lb (68kN)

Cylinder bore: 5$\frac{1}{2}$in (0.13m)
Cylinder stroke: 7$\frac{3}{4}$in (0.19m)
Transmission engine to gearbox: Fluidrive Type 23 HYD coupling
Transmission gearbox: Wilson-Drewry CAJ R7
Transmission final drive: SCG Type RF11
Gear ratio: First — 4.07:1
Second 2.33:1
Third — 1.55:1
Fourth — 1:1
Fifth — 1:1.87 OD
Fuel tank capacity: 300gal (1,364lit)
Cooling water capacity: 40gal (182lit)
Lub oil capacity: 8 gal (36lit)
Region of allocation: Eastern, Western Midland
Works responsible for classified overhauls: Doncaster, Swindon
* Locomotives allocated to LE for use on BPGV line are fitted with non-standard multiple system

Below:
This drawing represents a dual braked example, fitted with buffer beam air connections only; arrangement is the same for vacuum only examples except the air pipes and air tanks to the front of the cab windows are omitted. BPGV locomotives have a lower cab height, whilst others have duplicate air pipes at waist height.

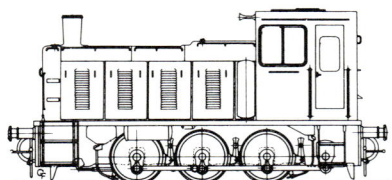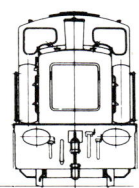

Left:
The once sizeable fleet of Class 03 shunting locomotives has diminished in recent years, with the withdrawal of the majority of vacuum brake only examples, leaving a handful of dual braked and very few vacuum only machines in traffic. In this view No 03.086 a dual braked example is shown, recognisable from a vacuum only locomotive by the additional air pipes on the buffer beam. This locomotive also has high level duplicate air connections. Colin J. Marsden

Right:
Nose end connections of dual braked example, with duplicate high-level air connections. On the rear of the locomotive connections will be the same, although mounted in slightly different positions. 1. High-level dual main reservoir/brake pipe cock, 2. Main reservoir pipe, 3. Brake pipe, 4. Vacuum pipe, 5. Nose end marker/rear lights (positions may vary).
Michael Collins

Below:
The cab or rear ends of two Class 03 locomotives are shown here. On the left No 03.066, a dual braked example, whilst on the right No 03.069 is a vacuum brake only locomotive. Standard livery for this fleet is BR rail blue with 'wasp' painted warning ends and black or yellow buffer beams (this being dependent on which BREL works undertook the last classified overhaul). Normally screw couplings are provided at each end of a locomotive but for some reason No 03.069 in this illustration has its coupling removed. Colin J. Marsden

Above:
To give access to the engine compartment four removable doors are placed on each side of the Class 03. If this does not facilitate access to the required component, the roof sections over the nose or bonnet part of the locomotive may also be removed. Dual braked No 03.399, the last locomotive of the type to be built, is illustrated here. The large cylindrical tank under the driving cab window is an air reservoir for the locomotive/train air braking system.   Colin J. Marsden

Below:
There is a significant detail difference with the seven Class 03s currently allocated to LE for use on the Burry Port & Gwendraeth Valley line. These examples have their cab height reduced by 4$\frac{7}{16}$in, enabling them to operate over the restricted clearance of the BPGV line. In addition to their cab height reduction, a headlight is fitted in front of the exhaust stack, required when locomotives cross unprotected level crossings. Two reduced height locomotives Nos 03.119/120 are shown here on shed at LE. The section of line over which these locomotives operate is scheduled for closure, rendering these locomotives surplus and candidates for withdrawal.   Andrew French

Above:
A recent Class 03 modification is the fitting of a yellow flashing light above the cab roof on Nos 03.179/399, enabling the locomotives to meet safety requirements for operating over the dock lines in the Ipswich area. Although these locomotives are allocated to Colchester depot where one can usually be found, the other is normally operating in the Ipswich area. The lamp can clearly be seen in this view of the locomotive on the stabling point. Colin J. Marsden

Below:
Due to difficulties in certain areas where Class 03 locomotives fail to operate track circuit equipment satisfactorily, match wagons are semi-permanently coupled to them. These match or shunting runner vehicles are usually former lowfit or conflat type wagons, vacuum or dual brake fitted, and classified under the TOPS system as ZSV or ZSX. Class 03 No 03.022 sporting twin warning horns and the older style tapered exhaust stack stands at Newcastle station coupled to ZSX No DB451897 during early 1982. Colin J. Marsden

Class 08

Number series: 08.001-08.954
Former number: D3000/D4192
Built by: BR at Derby/Crewe/Darlington/Doncaster and Horwich
Introduced: 1953-59
Type: 0-6-0
Weight in running order: 48-49 tonnes
Height: 12ft 8⅝in (3.87m)
Width: 8ft 6in (2.59m)
Length: 29ft 3in (8.91m)
Min curve negotiable: 3 chains (60.35m)
Maximum speed: 15-20mph (32km/h)
Wheelbase: 11ft 6in (3.50m)
Wheel diameter: 4ft 6in (1.37m)
Brake type: Air, vacuum, dual
Sanding equipment: Pneumatic
Route availability: 5
Brake force: 19 tonnes

Engine type: English Electric 6K
HP: 350hp (261kW)
Tractive effort: 35,000lb (156kN)
Cylinder bore: 10in (0.25m)
Cylinder stroke: 12in (0.30m)
Main generator type: EE801-8E
Aux generator type: EE736-2D
Traction motor type: EE506-6A or EE506-7C
Gear ratio: 23.9:1
Fuel tank capacity: 668gal (3,037lit)
Cooling water capacity: 140gal (636lit)
Lub oil capacity: 45gal (204lit)
Region of allocation: Eastern, Midland, Scottish, Southern, Western
Works responsible for classified overhauls: Doncaster, Eastleigh, Glasgow, Swindon

Below:
This drawing is representative of a vacuum braked only example. On dual or air brake fitted locomotives, the frame mounted equipment boxes may be of a revised layout, together with different piping arrangements on the buffer beam. For various details please see illustrations.

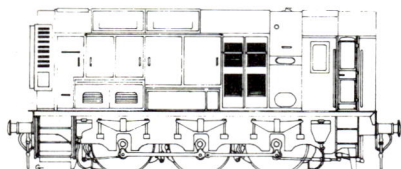
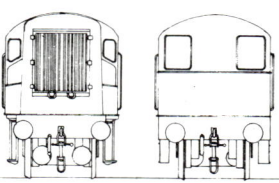

Left:
The standard shunting locomotive of today is the Class 08, whose design can be traced back well over 40 years to the LMS designs of the late 1930s and early 1940s. This once numerous fleet, which numbered nearly 1,000, has been eroded in recent years, with many examples being withdrawn as surplus to requirements, this mainly confined to vacuum brake only locomotives. Vacuum brake only No 08.008 (now withdrawn) is shown here, recognisable from other brake fitted types by having only a vacuum hose and coupling on the buffer beam.
Colin J. Marsden

Above:
In 1959 the BR workshops at Crewe built vacuum braked No 08.580 shown here. This side view shows the various body side doors which open on hinges or can be removed to give access to engine room equipment. Three boxes can be seen on the frame plate towards the nose end of the locomotive, these contain the main battery isolating switch (left), batteries (middle), and air compressor (right). On the cab end only two marker lights remain, although the locomotive would have been built with six.
Colin J. Marsden

Right:
Front end layout of equipment on dual brake fitted Class 08. This arrangement is also applicable to Class 09 locomotives. 1. Main reservoir air pipe, 2. Brake pipe, 3. Vacuum pipe, 4. Radiator water filler points, 5. Radiator water level gauge, 6. Radiator shutter handle, 7. Front/Rear marker lights (able to show white or red). The locomotive illustrated here at Perth is No 08.762
David Nicholas

Above:
All Class 08 locomotives were either built as plain vacuum brake fitted, or given the extra and rather useful facility of being dual braked (air/vacuum), but in more recent years, with the elimination of a number of vacuum braked services, the need for vacuum brake fitted locomotives has largely diminished. This in turn has led to a sizeable number of locomotives passing through works to be fitted with air brake equipment only; these are recognisable by the omission of the vacuum pipe from the buffer beams. Air brake only No 08.504 is illustrated here. Colin J. Marsden

Below:
Perhaps the most useful breed of Class 08 shunter is that fitted with dual (air/vacuum) brake equipment. Whilst it is not possible for a train to be operated formed of a mixture of air/vacuum stock with brakes operating, the dual facility is very useful, particularly where station pilot duties are involved, enabling the locomotive to shunt either air or vacuum stock. The changeover between the two systems only needs the turn of an electric switch in the cab. DB No 08.756, fitted with duplicate high-level pipes, stands at Bristol on 10 November 1981. Colin J. Marsden

Above:
Front end layout of dual braked Class 08 with additional high-level duplicate air pipes. The duplication of high-level air pipes are particularly common amongst shunters allocated to the SR, or in areas where coupling to electric multiple unit stock fitted with waist level air connections may be necessary. This illustration shows No 08.837 standing at Stewarts Lane with four front end marker lights, although those at top middle, and centre bottom have been blanked out of use.   Colin J. Marsden

Below:
Various cab door detail differences exist within the Class 08 fleet, the majority of older examples have wooden doors with one central brass handle, whereas later locomotives have an all steel door with two handles, enabling it to be opened from ground level. Due to replacements and shopping of locomotives over the years some are in traffic with different door designs on each side. No 08.940 sports an all steel door in this view taken at Severn Tunnel Junction depot during 1981.   Colin J. Marsden

Above:
An interesting fitment made to No 08.822 of CF depot is a large headlight, carried on the central lamp iron on the radiator grille, this has been fitted as the locomotive's duties involve operating in Newport docks where unprotected crossings exist, and also in the BSC works at Llanwern. The locomotive is seen here departing from the BSC works with an empty coal train during November 1981.   Colin J. Marsden

Below:
During the early 1980s a number of air brake only, and dual brake Class 08s have been fitted with dropable buck-eye couplings, for use in shunting IC125 power cars and vehicles. Buck-eye fitted members are recognisable by having the buck-eye head hanging on the coupling shank, and the omission of the standard screw coupling, however these locomotives may be used as conventional shunters, by using the link coupling from another vehicle or a 'loose' coupling held at the depot. No 08.480 stands outside Old Oak Common factory sporting the 125 legend on its battery box.
Colin J. Marsden

Above:
Although the Class 253/4 DM/DMB cars are capable of moving themselves when single, for transfer between depots and adjoining workshops, cars are usually hauled by one of the allocation of buck-eye fitted Class 08 locomotives. Here Bristol allocated No 08.483 hauls DMB No 43047 towards Bristol Bath Road maintenance depot from the nearby St Phillips Marsh HST Depot. Colin J. Marsden

Below:
Over recent years several depots have unofficially added names to their shunting locomotives, some with the blessing of local management but others indeed not so! For station pilot duties at Plymouth, LA allocated No 08.953 was adorned with Plymouth *plates during 1981. Although resembling the official type of some years ago the nameplates were constructed locally by the LA depot staff.* Colin J. Marsden

Class 09

Number series: 09.001-09.026
Former number: D3665-3671, 3719-3721, 4099-4114
Built by: BR at Darlington and Horwich
Introduced: From 1954
Type: 0-6-0
Weight in running order: 49 tonnes
Height: 12ft 8⅝in (3.87m)
Width: 8ft 10in (2.69m)
Length: 29ft 3in (8.91m)
Min curve negotiable: 3½ chains (70.40m)
Maximum speed: 27mph (34km/h)
Wheelbase: 11ft 6in (3.50m)
Wheel diameter: 4ft 6in (1.37m)
Brake type: Dual
Sanding equipment: Pneumatic
Route availability: 5
Brake force: 19 tonnes

Engine type: English Electric 6K
HP: 350hp (261kW)
Tractive effort: 35,000lb (156kN)
Cylinder bore: 10in (0.25m)
Cylinder stroke: 12in (0.30m)
Main generator type: English Electric 801.8E
Aux generator type: English Electric 736.2D
Traction motor type: English Electric 506.6A or 506.7C
Gear ratio: 23.9:1
Fuel tank capacity: 668gal (3,036lit)
Cooling water capacity: 140gal (636lit)
Lub oil capacity: 45gal (205lit)
Region of allocation: Southern
Works responsible for classified overhauls: Eastleigh

Below:
This drawing is representative of the majority of the fleet; all locomotives are fitted with dual brake equipment and high level extension pipes. Differences may occur in end fittings. This drawing has been prepared to the original condition of the locomotive, with a ladder on the nose end by the side of the radiator.

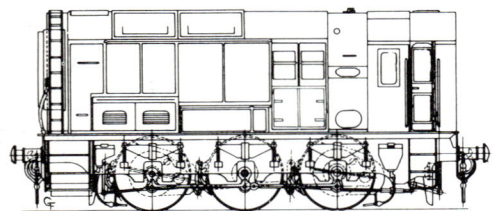 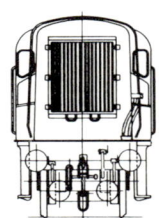

Left:
The only major difference between a Class 08 fitted with dual brake equipment, and a Class 09, is the additional air compressor in an external box in front of the fuel tank, which is situated to the front of the driving position. This compressor is only used when the driver selects an 'air' position on the brake selector switch for hauling air braked trains. A single air compressor internally mounted, is otherwise sufficient to provide the normal air supply for the locomotive. Nose end equipment is identical to Class 08 DB fitted locomotives. Colin J. Marsden

Above:
All Class 09 locomotives are allocated to the SR and fitted with dual brake equipment, with additional high-level air connections. Another difference between the Class 08s and 09s is the maximum speed. Class 08s are restricted to only 15mph whereas Class 09s are permitted to travel at up to 27mph; if this speed is exceeded an automatic overspeed device will operate and apply the auto brake to the locomotive and train. No 09.003 stands next to a Class 33/0 at Norwood on 5 March 1982.
Colin J. Marsden

Right:
*Cab end layout of Class 09 (also applicable for dual braked Class 08 locomotives with additional high-level air pipes).
1. High-level dual main reservoir/brake pipe cock, 2. Main reservoir pipe, 3. Brake pipe, 4. Vacuum pipe, 5. Fuel entry equipment, 6. Head/tail marker lights (capable of showing white/red).*
Colin J. Marsden

Class 13

Number series: 13.001-13.003
Former number: D4500-D4502
Built by: BR Darlington*
Introduced: 1965
Type: 0-6-0+0-6-0
Weight in running order: 120 tonnes
Height: 12ft 8⅝in (3.87m)
Width: 8ft 6in (2.59m)
Length: 60ft 1in (18.31m)
Min curve negotiable: 2½ chains (50.29m)
Maximum speed: 20mph (32km/h)
Wheelbase (total): 42ft 1½in (12.83m)
Wheel diameter: 4ft 6in (1.37m)
Brake type: Vacuum
Sanding equipment: Pneumatic
Route availability: 8
Brake force: 38 tonnes
Engine type: 2×English Electric 6K
HP (total): 700hp (521kW)

Tractive effort: 32,000lb (142kN)
Cylinder bore: 10in (0.25m)
Cylinder stroke: 12in (0.30m)
Main generator type: English Electric 801-8E
Aux generator type: English Electric 736-2D
Traction motor type: English Electric 506-6A
Gear ratio: 23.9:1
Fuel tank capacity (total): 1,336gal (6,073lit)
Cooling water capacity (total): 280gal (1,273lit)
Lub oil capacity (total): 90gal (409lit)
Region of allocation: Eastern
Works responsible for classified overhauls: Swindon
* Converted from Class 08.

Below:
This drawing shows the present coupling arrangement for these locomotives, the only formation now permitted. When introduced, the Class 13s were coupled cab to cab.

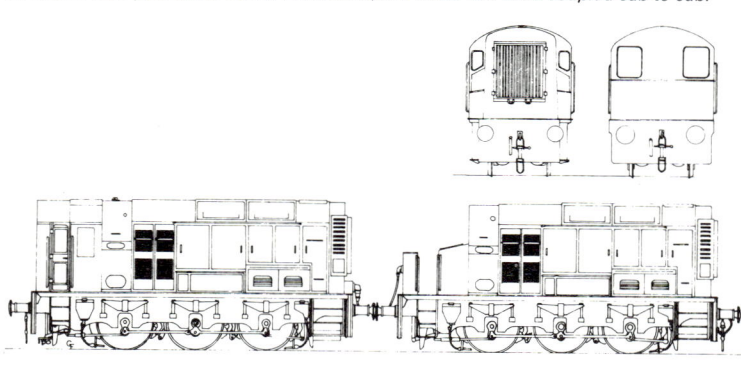

Bottom left:
One of the most unusual shunter type locomotives ever introduced was the three master and slave units converted from standard Class 08s, for use in the modern marshalling yards at Tinsley, near Sheffield, where high powered locomotives were needed to propel long and extremely heavy trains up the 'hump' gradients. During conversion work each new locomotive was converted from two Class 08s, one locomotive from each pair having its cab removed to become the Slave; power and control given to the remaining complete locomotive, the Master, by means of control jumpers. Due to the high adhesion required additional weight was needed, being provided by enlarging the buffer beams in depth and thickness. No 13.001 shown from the master unit end stands at Tinsley fuelling point during 1982. Colin J. Marsden

Above:
Coupling detail between Master (on right) and Slave (on left). 1. Control jumper, 2. Engine control air pipe, 3. Vacuum pipe, 4. Main reservoir pipe, 5. Brake pipe, 6. Fuel entry equipment (for Slave unit only), 7. Control jumper dummy receptacle.
Steve Montgomery

Below:
Although three Class 13 locomotives were built, only two now remain in use, the third, No 13.002, was withdrawn during 1981 and subsequently scrapped at Swindon. The two remaining locomotives are also candidates for early withdrawal following the general decline in wagon load traffic. Withdrawn No 13.002 stands outside Tinsley depot during 1980. The extended buffer beam can clearly be seen in this illustration. Class 13s carry radio-telephone equipment, enabling the driver to speak with Tinsley control tower during hump shunting. Steve Montgomery

Class 20

Number series: 20.001-20.199, 20.200-20.228
Former number: D8000-D8199, D8300-D8327
Built by: English Electric Vulcan Foundry and Robert Stevenson & Hawthorn
Introduced: From 1957
Type: Bo-Bo
Weight in running order: 72 tonnes
Height: 12ft 7⅝in (3.84m)
Width: 8ft 9in (2.66m)
Length: 46ft 9¼in (14.26m)
Min curve negotiable: 3½ chains (70.40m)
Maximum speed: 75mph (121km/h)
Wheelbase: 32ft 6in (9.90m)
Bogie wheel base: 8ft 6in (2.59m)
Bogie pivot centres: 24ft 0in (7.31m)
Wheel diameter: 3ft 7in (1.09m)
Brake type: Vacuum, dual
Sanding equipment: Pneumatic
Route availability: 5

Coupling restriction: Blue Star
Brake force: 35 tonnes
Engine type: English Electric 8SVT MKII
HP: 1,000hp (745kW)
Tractive effort: 42,000lb (187kN)
Cylinder bore: 10in (0.25m)
Cylinder stroke: 12in (0.30m)
Main generator type: English Electric 819/3C
Aux generator type: English Electric 991/2B
Traction motor type: English Electric 526/5D
Gear ratio: 63:17
Fuel tank capacity: 380gal (1,727lit)
Cooling water capacity: 130gal (591lit)
Lub oil capacity: 100gal (455lit)
Region of allocation: Eastern, Midland, Scottish
Works responsible for classified overhauls: Crewe, Glasgow

Below:
The first 128 Class 20 locomotives were built with the disc train identification system, similar to that used on steam traction. The Class 20s are immediately recognisable from all other main line classes by having the driving cab at one end only, with a long nose bonnet resembling a large Class 08 or 09. No 20.011 is shown here at Tinsley.
Colin J. Marsden

No. 1 END.

No. 2 END.

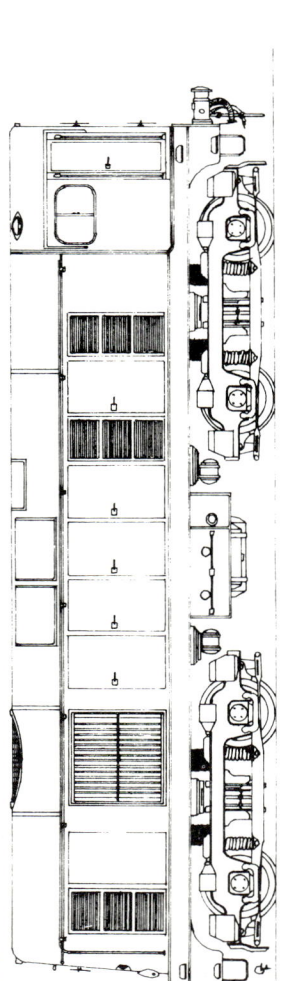

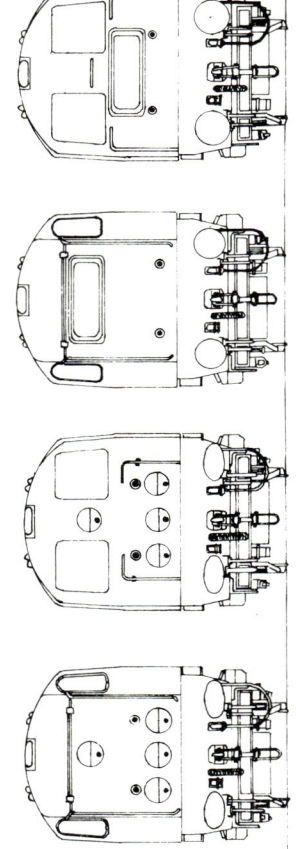

Above:
This side elevation is representative of locomotives Nos 20.001-20.128 fitted with the disc train identification system. Four nose/rear ends are shown, the disc ends are carried on locomotives Nos 20.001-128 and the four position route indicator style ends on Nos 20.129-228. It will be noted that different style buffers are shown, although it is not constant that disc headcoded examples carry oval buffers and headcode box members the round style. One locomotive has been observed in traffic with round buffers on one end and oval at the other!

21

Right:
Cab end layout of disc headcoded Class 20, fitted with dual brakes. 1. Engine control air pipe, 2. Main reservoir pipe, 3. Brake pipe, 4. Vacuum pipe, 5. Multiple-unit (Blue Star) control jumper receptacle, 6. Multiple-unit (Blue Star) control jumper cable, 7. AWS receiving equipment, 8. Red electric tail indicator, 9. White frontal indicators (one behind each disc, when open), 10. Two-tone warning horns (under grille). Note: On vacuum braked only locomotives, the brake pipe (No 3) would be omitted. Colin J. Marsden

Below:
Two brake types exist within Class 20 — those locomotives fitted with vacuum brakes, and those with dual air/vacuum equipment. Recognition between the two types is best achieved by reference to the buffer beam to see if an air brake pipe is carried. After 128 locomotives had been built the nose and cab ends were revised to accommodate the four character route identification system which, in recent years, has been displaced by two white marker discs. No 20.211 is shown at Barrow Hill. Colin J. Marsden

Right:
Except in the area of the cooler group (grilles on side towards front of loco) access can be gained to the power unit, generator and associated equipment via nine hinged doors on each side of the bonnet section; these doors can also be removed if more convenient. This illustration serves as good comparison of two of the modernisation Type 1 single cab locomotives, behind Class 20 No 20.151, is a former BTH Class 15 locomotive, later used as an electric train heating generator. Derek Porter

Right:
Above: A handful of the Class 20 fleet are fitted with three piece miniature snowploughs, however mounting brackets are fitted to the majority of the class. These ploughs are usually painted yellow and would be able to move small amounts of snow, approximately up to 10in. For large accumulations one of the independent snowploughs or a locomotive fitted with snow-wings would be required.
No 20.141 is seen here at March during early 1982.
Michael Collins

Right:
A nose end modification to at least one ScR allocated member No 20.028 was recorded during early 1983 — the fitting of a large snowplough on the nose end buffer beam in place of buffers; in fact this attachment is secured to the locomotive by the buffer mounting points.
No 20.028 was photographed at Eastfield depot, but it was not reported whether this fitment was used during the adverse conditions of the 1982-3 winter.
Steve Montgomery

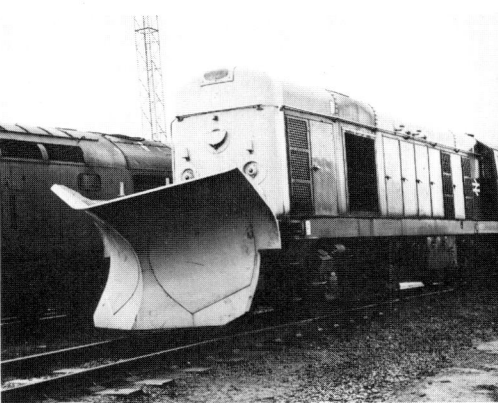

Class 25

Number series: 25.001-25.327
Former number: D5151-D5299, D7500-D7677
Built by: BR at Derby, Darlington, Crewe and Beyer Peacock Ltd, Gorton
Introduced: 1961-1967
Type: Bo-Bo
Weight in running order: 73t 15cwt (73.9 tonnes)
Height: 12ft 8in (3.86m)
Width: 9ft 1in (2.76m)
Length: 50ft 6in (15.39m)
Min curve negotiable: 4½ chains (90.52m)
Maximum speed: 90mph (145km/h)
Wheelbase: 36ft 6in (11.12m)
Bogie wheel base: 8ft 6in (2.59m)
Bogie pivot centres: 28ft 0in (8.53m)
Wheel diameter — driving: 3ft 9in (1.14m)
Brake type: Vacuum, dual
Sanding equipment: Pneumatic
Heating type: Steam — Stones L4610 (if fitted)

Route availability: 5
Coupling restriction: Blue Star
Brake force: 38 tonnes
Engine type: Sulzer 6LDA28B
HP: 1,250hp (931kW)
Tractive effort: 45,000lb (200kN)
Cylinder bore: 11in (0.27m)
Cylinder stroke: 14in (0.35m)
Main generator type: AEI RTB 15656
Aux generator type: AEI RTB 7440
Traction motor type: AEI 253AY or AEI 137BK
Gear ratio: 18:67
Fuel tank capacity: 500gal (2,273lit)
Cooling water capacity: 187gal (850lit)
Boiler water capacity (if fitted): 580gal (2,651lit)
Lub oil capacity: 100gal (455lit)
Boiler fuel capacity (if fitted): From main supply
Region of allocation: Midland
Works responsible for classified overhauls: Derby

Below:
There are presently three sub-types of Class 25 in service: 25/1, 25/2 and 25/3, differences being in electrical and technical equipment. However two different body designs are used, but are not constant with the sub-classifications. Due to different works building batches of Class 25 locomotives concurrently, some design differences occur, out of number sequence. The main differences are therefore given:
25.027-082: Front gangway, side grilles on body.
25.083-217: No front gangway, side grilles at cant rail height.
25.218-247: Front gangway, side grilles on body.
25.248-327: No front gangway, side grilles at cant rail height.
Due to classified overhauls and collision repairs some locomotives are fitted with cabs from different builds. Class 25/1 No 25.059 with sealed up nose corridor gangway connection is show here. Between the bogies are the batteries with fuel tank underneath and boiler water tank adjacent.   Steve Montgomery

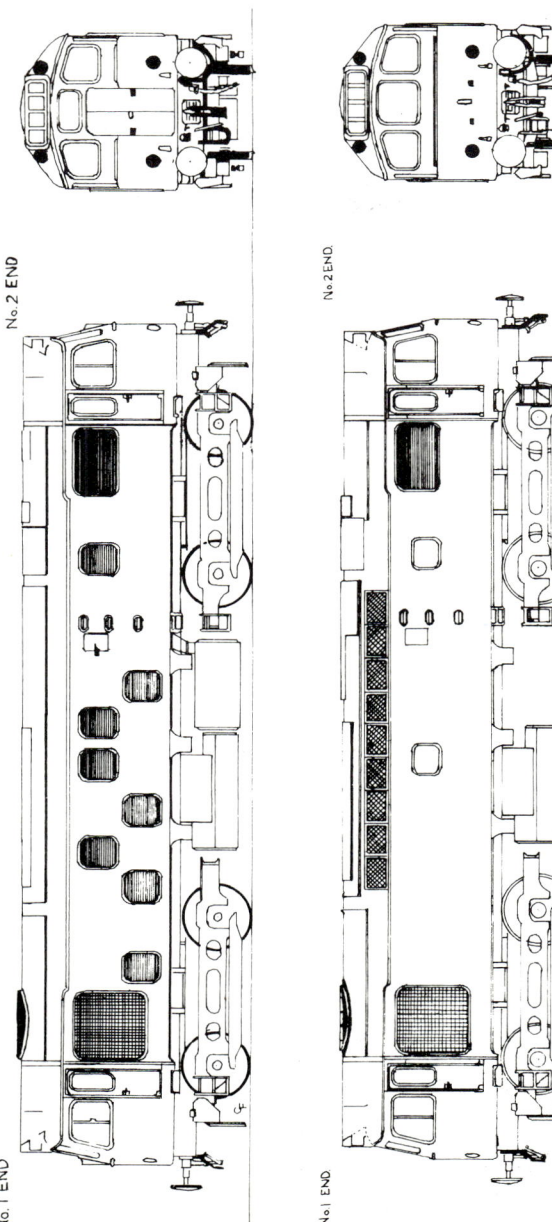

No. 1 END

No. 2 END

No. 1 END

No. 2 END

Above:

The upper drawing represents the arrangement on locomotives Nos 25.027-082/ 25.218-247 fitted with steam heating facilities (boiler water tank on underframe). The lower drawing is representative of Nos 25.083-217/25.248-327 with revised body side arrangement and air vents grouped at cant rail height. The lower drawing shows a locomotive not fitted for steam heat operation (omission of boiler water tank on underframe).

Above:
Front end detail of the two different Class 25 nose end designs. 1. Main reservoir pipe, 2. Brake pipe (only carried on dual brake fitted locomotives), 3. Engine control air pipe, 4. Vacuum pipe, 5. Multiple control (Blue Star) jumper cable, 6. Multiple control (Blue Star) jumper socket, 7. Steam pipe, 8. Red tail indicator light, 9. Two tone warning horns, 10. Front end marker lights. On the left is the front of VB 25/1 No 25.069, while on the right DB 25/2 No 25.182. Both Colin J. Marsden

Below:
This view of the stabling point at Skipton gives a good comparison of the two body designs. Initially under the modernisation plan corridor connections were to be fitted to all main line locomotives enabling crew changes en route, however after only a short period this was deemed unnecessary and removed from subsequent orders. At the same time the body sides were cleaned up with the eight former side mounted air vents being repositioned in a neat bank at cant rail height. Class 25/2 No 25.229 fitted with steam heat equipment is on the left, whilst '25/2' No 25.138 is on the right with no boiler water tank on the underframe, indicating the locomotive is not heat fitted.
Colin J. Marsden

Above:
General view of early designed locomotive taken from the No 1 end with the coolant and radiator group nearest the camera. It will be seen that the roof is divided into three sections, one over each of the coolant, engine/generator and boiler compartments. All roof sections are removable to give good access to all equipment. Colin J. Marsden

Below:
With revised air ventilation on later locomotives it became possible for two small windows to be fixed into the engine compartment, vastly improving working conditions in the engine room. Again photographed from No 1 end, Class 25/3 No 25.251 stands in Willesden Brent Sidings. Colin J. Marsden

Above:
View of Class 25/3 locomotive from No 2 end with the boiler compartment nearest the camera. Although this locomotive is not fitted with train heating equipment (no boiler water tank or steam pipe), the plate directly behind the driver's assistant's position covers a boiler compartment vent (on some locomotives this may be uncovered). Dual brake fitted No 25.303 stands at Crewe on 19 February 1982. Ian Gould

Below:
Three piece miniature snowploughs are fitted to a number of locomotives. While the majority of locomotives have mounting brackets, during 1982/3 some locomotives were seen sporting larger snowploughs mounted on the buffer beam in place of buffers. No 25.138 is seen at Skipton after duties utilising the miniature snowplough on the Settle & Carlisle route during February 1983. Colin J. Marsden

Above:
Allocation of the entire Class 25 fleet is now to the LMR, but visits of the class to WR, ER and ScR are not uncommon with many drivers on these regions still trained in their use. One stronghold for the class for many years was on the Crewe-Cardiff route and it is on this service we see now withdrawn Class 25/1 No 25.043 near Newport during July 1980. Colin J. Marsden

Below: *With major body alterations carried out to later locomotives an improvement to cab comfort was made possible, with the elimination of the nose corridor doors a larger centre window could be fitted, giving increased light to the cab. Here Class 25/2 No 25.101 stands coupled to Class 25/2 No 25.286 at Nuneaton at the head of a southbound coal train.* Colin J. Marsden

Class 26

Number series: 26.001-26.046
Former number: D5300-D5346
Built by: Birmingham Railway
Carriage & Wagon Ltd
Introduced: From 1958
Type: Bo-Bo
Weight in running order: 77t 10cwt
(77.6 tonnes)
Height: 12ft 8in (3.86m)
Width: 8ft 10in (2.69m)
Length: 50ft 9in (15.46m)
Min curve negotiable: 5 chains
(100.58m)
Maximum speed: 75mph (121km/h)
Wheelbase: 39ft 0in (11.88m)
Bogie wheelbase: 10ft 0in (3.04m)
Bogie pivot centres: 29ft 0in (8.83m)
Wheel diameter — driving: 3ft 7in
(1.09m)
Brake type: Vacuum, dual
Sanding equipment: Pneumatic
Heating type: Steam Stones OK4616
Route availability: 6 (26001-26020)
5 (26021-26046)

Coupling restriction: Blue Star
Brake force: 35 tonnes
Engine type: Sulzer 6LDA28A
HP: 1,160hp (864kW)
Tractive effort: 42,000lb (187kN)
Cylinder bore: 11in (0.27m)
Cylinder stroke: 14in (0.35m)
Main generator type: CG 391/A1
Aux generator type: CAG 193/1A
Traction motor type: C171Al 26001-
26007, C171D3 26008-26046
C171D3 26008-26046
Gear ratio: 63:16
Fuel tank capacity: 500gal (2,273lit)
Cooling water capacity: 190gal
(864lit)
Boiler water capacity: 550gal
(2,500lit)
Lub oil capacity: 100gal (455lit)
Boiler fuel capacity: From main suply
Region of allocation: Scottish
**Works responsible for classified
overhauls:** Glasgow

Below:
*There are two sub-classes of the Class 26 locomotive in service — Class 26/0, the first
seven members of this sub-class are used almost exclusively for freight traffic and are
fitted with dual brakes. Class 26/0 is recognised by an air compressor mounted on the
under-frame in place of the boiler water tank. No 26.006 stands at Millerhill, a
stronghold for the class.* Steve Montgomery

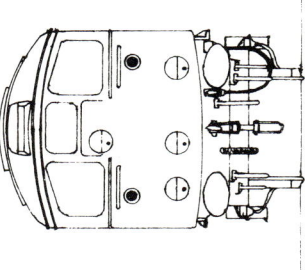

N° 1 END

N° 2 END.

Above:
Two different Class 26 designs are currently in traffic; this drawing is representative of locomotives Nos 26.008-019, fitted with leaf secondary springing, oval buffers, steam heating and multiple-unit equipment mounted on the buffer beam.

31

Left and below:
Front end detail of Class 26/0 locomotive on the left, and Class 26/1 below: 1. Engine control air pipe, 2. Main reservoir pipe, 3. Vacuum pipe, 4. Steam pipe, 5. Multiple control (Blue Star) jumper cable. 6. Multiple control (Blue Star) jumper socket. 7. AWS receiving apparatus, 8. Red tail indicator light. Note: Class 26/0 has oval buffers, but Class 26/1 has round.
Both David Nicholas

Top right:
Detail differences exist in cab side windows, buffing gear, springing, and multiple control gear. Locomotives Nos 26.001-019 were built with drop light windows, oval buffers, leaf secondary springing and multiple-unit control jumpers mounted on the buffer beam. These detail differences can be easily recognised if this and the following plate are compared. No 26.014 is illustrated from No 1 end. Ian Gould

Right:
As much of the work undertaken by Class 26 locomotives takes them over unprotected crossings, a number have been fitted with headlights. Two types are known to exist with a single, or double lamp, in a fixed beam pattern and are normally to be found mid-way up the former corridor connection door. Another recent modification on some locomotives is the removal of some or all former train identification discs. Some discs have been removed from No 26.021 illustrated here.
David Nicholas

Right:
A large number of Class 26 locomotives are fitted with three-piece miniature snowploughs usually painted yellow, but black livery has also been recorded. It is understood that many of the earlier locomotives built with drop light windows will have these replaced with the sliding type, as and when they pass through main works for classified overhaul. In resplendent condition No 26.040 sporting slightly larger numerals than standard (a trademark of BREL Glasgow) stands at Inverness during 1981.
Andrew French

Class 27

Number series: 27.001-27.066
Former number: D5347-D5415
Built by: Birmingham Railway Carriage & Works
Introduced: 1961-62
Type: Bo-Bo
Weight in running order: Various between 71-76 tonnes
Height: 12ft 8in (3.86m)
Width: 8ft 10in (2.69m)
Length: 50ft 9in (15.46m)
Min curve negotiable: 5 chains (100.58m)
Maximum speed: 90mph (145km/h)
Wheelbase: 39ft 0in (11.88m)
Bogie wheelbase: 10ft 0in (3.04m)
Bogie pivot centres: 29ft 0in (8.83m)
Wheel diameter — driving: 3ft 7in (1.09m)
Brake type: Vacuum, dual
Sanding equipment: Pneumatic
Heating type if fitted: Steam — Stones OK 4625

Route availability: 5
Coupling restriction: Blue Star
Brake force: 35 tonnes
Engine type: Sulzer 6LDA28B
HP: 1,250hp (931kW)
Tractive effort: 40,000lb (178kN)
Cylinder bore: 11in (0.27m)
Cylinder stroke: 14in (0.35m)
Main generator type: GEC WT981
Aux generator type: GEC WT782
Traction motor type: GEC WT459
Gear ratio: 60:17
Fuel tank capacity: 685gal (3,114lit)
Cooling water capacity: 190gal (864lit)
Boiler water capacity (if fitted): 300gal (1,354lit)
Lub oil capacity: 100gal (455lit)
Boiler fuel capacity (if fitted): From main supply
Region of allocation: Scottish
Works responsible for classified overhauls: Glasgow

Below:
To many enthusiasts the Class 26 and 27 are identical, but many detail differences exist. For recognition purposes the easiest way to detect a Class 27 is by the omission of the disc headcode system and the presence of a headcode box on the cab roof. All Class 27 locomotives were built with the facility to have nose corridor connections but these have since been removed. Here the first member of the class, No 27.001 stands at Ayr on 22 March 1980.   Steve Montgomery

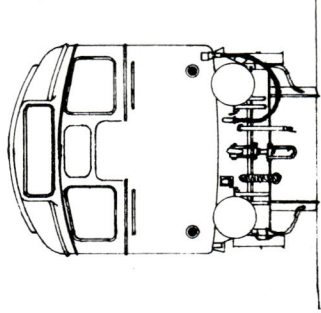

Above:
Representative of the majority of Class 27 locomotives, drop light style cab windows are shown, although a number of locomotives now have the sliding type. Window layout on both sides of the body are identical.

35

Left and below:
Front end detail and close-up of buffer beam area on Class 27 locomotive. The full front illustration shows a dual brake example, whilst the detail view illustrates a vacuum only member. 1. Main reservoir pipe, 2. Control air pipe, 3. Vacuum pipe, 4. Steam pipe, 5. Brake pipe (dual brake fitted locomotives only), 6. Multiple control (Blue Star) jumper socket, 7. Multiple control (Blue Star) jumper cable. 8. Red tail indicator light.
Colin J. Marsden/David Nicholas

Above:
Locomotive Nos 27.024-031, 27.045, when built during the early 1960s were allocated to English depots for freight work only, and not given a provision for train heating. However, after their transfer to Scotland one locomotive now numbered 27.045, was given steam heat equipment by Glasgow works. The remaining locomotives are always recognisable by the large space on their underframe where the boiler water tank would have been placed. This is clearly visible on this view of No 27.025. David Nicholas

Below:
Initially the first 23 locomotives were built with sliding cab side windows, whilst the remainder of the class had drop light windows. However in recent years, following the heavy general overhaul of some locomotives, sliding windows are becoming the norm. No heat fitted No 27.030 is viewed from the No 2 end in this illustration taken at Eastfield depot. David Nicholas

Note: During late 1970 it was decided to modify a batch of 24 Class 27 locomotives for air brake operation and fit a method of through train control to enable a push-pull system to operate between Edinburgh and Glasgow, with a locomotive at each end of a rake of Mk 2 coaches. Locomotives so treated were reclassified '27/1', all modifications being internal. Soon after passenger services commenced it was decided to convert 12 of the Class 27/1 locomotives for electric train heat operation. This was achieved by fitting a small engine and generator in the position formerly occupied by the boiler. These locomotives were classified as '27/2'. Following the introduction of revised push-pull services on the Edinburgh-Glasgow line from the late 1970s using Class 47/7 locomotives, the push-pull and ETH equipment was deemed redundant and subsequently removed, thus returning the locomotives to their Class 27/0 status. Removal of equipment and locomotive renumbering commenced at the end of 1982.

Class 31

Number series: 31.101-31.327, 31.401-31.440
Former number: D5500-D5699, D5800-D5862
Built by: Brush Ltd
Introduced: From 1957
Type: A1A-A1A
Weight in running order: Between 107 113 tonnes various
Height: 12ft 7in (3.83m)
Width: 8ft 9in (2.66m)
Length: 56ft 9in (17.29m)
Min curve negotiable: 4½ chains (90.52m)
Maximum speed: 80mph* (129km/h), 90mph† (145km/h)
Wheelbase: 42ft 10in (13.05m)
Bogie wheelbase: 14ft 0in (4.26m)
Bogie pivot centres: 28ft 10in (8.78m)
Wheel diameter — driving: 3ft 7in (1.09m)
Wheel diameter — centre: 3ft 3½in (1.00m)
Brake type: Vacuum, dual. Some vacuum locos fitted with EQ brake
Sanding equipment: Pneumatic
Heating type: 31/1 Steam — Spanner Mk 1

31/4 Electric or dual
Route availability: 5
Coupling restriction: Blue Star
Brake force: 49 tonnes
Engine type: English Electric 12SVT
HP: 1,470hp (1,095kW)
Tractive effort: 42,800lb* (190kN), 35,900lb† (160kN)
Cylinder bore: 10in (0.25m)
Cylinder stroke: 12in (0.30m)
Main generator type: Brush TG160.48
Aux generator type: Brush TG69.42
Traction motor type: Brush TM73.68
Gear ratio: 64:15*, 60:19†
Fuel tank capacity: 530gal (2,409lit)
Cooling water capacity: 156gal (709lit)
Boiler water capacity: 600gal (2,728lit)
Lub oil capacity: 110gal (500lit)
Boiler fuel capacity: 100gal (455lit)
Region of allocation: Eastern, Midland, Western
Works responsible for classified overhauls: Doncaster
* 31.101-31.116
†31.117-31.440

Below:
Two basic types of Class 31 are presently in traffic. Locomotives with either vacuum or dual brake and fitted with or without steam heating are classified as '31/1', whilst those fitted with electric or dual heating and dual braking are classified as '31/4'. Class 31/1 No 31.260 fitted for vacuum brake operation and steam heating stands with No 1 end nearest the camera. Colin J. Marsden

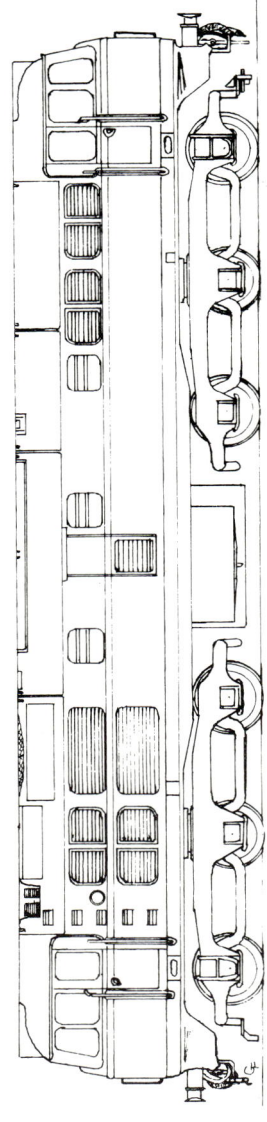

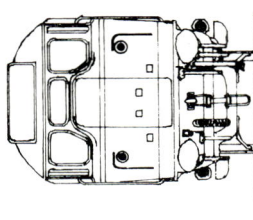

Above:

This drawing is representative of a Class 31/1 locomotive of the batch fitted with four position route indicators. This modification was progressively adopted from No 31.113 and fitted to all locomotives after No 31.143. Class 31/4s fitted with electric train heating (ETH) equipment have additional jumpers mounted on the buffer beam front end. Note the footsteps to the roof boiler water filling point — these have now been plated over on most examples.

Above:
Front end layouts: on the left dual braked steam heat locomotive '31/1' and on the right a dual braked, dual heat locomotive '31/4'. Note: On vacuum brake only locomotives the main reservoir pipe (No 3) will not be carried. 1. Engine control air pipe, 2. Main reservoir pipe, 3. Air brake pipe, 4. Vacuum pipe, 5. Steam pipe, 6. Multiple control (Blue Star) jumper socket, 7. Multiple control (Blue Star) jumper cable, 8. ETH jumper socket, 9. ETH jumper cable, 10. Red tail light, 11. Frontal marker light. Both these locomotives have had their former corridor connections sealed up — the 31/1 by a plate retaining the foot holes and the 31/4 by a new solid plate.
Both: Colin J. Marsden

Below:
Two Class 31 front end types exist. When the initial order for these Type 2 locomotives were made the four character identification system was not in use and train type identification was by marker light or disc by day. All the pioneer class 31/0 (electro magnetic) locomotives — now extinct — had disc headcodes, which continued with production locomotives as far as No 31.113, after which the new four position system was gradually adopted and introduced to some of the 31.113-142 batch. Thereafter all locomotives had the four position system. No 31.106 with some discs removed, stands at March in 1982. Colin J. Marsden

Above:
Side detail, Class 31/1, also applicable to Class 31/4, No 1 end on left. 1. Sand box, 2. Primary springing, 3. Secondary springing, 4. Brake cylinder, 5. Battery box, 6. Boiler water gauge, 7. Radiator grille, 8. Removable roof hatch (over power unit) 9. Engine exhaust, 10. Fire alarm pull.   Colin J. Marsden

Above:
Electric or dual heat Class 31s classified as sub-section four, are recognisable by the additional ETH jumper cable and socket on the buffer beam and front end. Up to 1982, 24 locomotives were so fitted, but with electrically heated rolling stock being more widely used, further steam heat examples were under conversion to ETH at BREL Doncaster works during 1983/84.
Colin J. Marsden

Left:
Many classes, including some Class 31s, carry snowploughs of the three part miniature type, however unlike others the Class 31 fitting does not remain constant and changes occur regularly. Ploughs are usually painted yellow. Plough fitted No 31.312 stands at Bristol Temple Meads. Colin J. Marsden

Above:
The Class 31/1 allocation is shared between the Eastern, Western and London Midland Regions, with ER having by far the largest number. The Class 31s are a truly mixed traffic type being diagrammed for passenger and freight duties. No 31.318 approaches Rotherham with the 07.00 Bristol-Leeds.   Colin J. Marsden

Below:
Class 31/4 locomotives are currently allocated to the Eastern Region at MR, TI, HM, and IM sheds and are normally found on passenger workings, often operating on to the LMR. No 31.411 illustrated here is an exception to the standard numbering rule by having numbers at each corner; it stands at Leeds with stock to form an overnight service to London.   Colin J. Marsden

Note: The standard livery for Class 31s is BR rail blue with full yellow ends, as illustrated. Some modifications do exist, one locomotive has yellow surrounds to the cab side windows and several have gained silver body stripes on the central coach line.

Class 33

Number series: 33.001-33.065,
33.101-33.119, 33.201-33.212
Former number: D6500-D6597
Built by: Birmingham Railway Carriage
& Wagon Co Ltd
Introduced: From 1959
Type: Bo-Bo
Weight in running order: Various
between 76/77 tonnes
Height: 12ft 8in (3.86m)
Width: 33/0, 33/1— 9ft 3in (2.81m)
33/2 — 6ft 8in (2.64m)
Length: 50ft 9in (15.46m)
Min curve negotiable: 4 chains
(80.46m)
Maximum speed: 85mph (137km/h)
Wheelbase: 39ft 0in (11.88m)
Bogie wheelbase: 10ft 0in (3.04m)
Bogie pivot centres: 29ft 0in (8.83m)
Wheel diameter — driving: 3ft 7in
(1.09m)
Brake type: Dual
Sanding equipment: Pneumatic

Heating type: Electric Index No 48
Route availability: 6
Coupling restriction: Blue Star
Brake force: 35 tonnes
Engine type: Sulzer 8LDA28
HP: 1,550hp (1,154kW)
Tractive effort: 45,000lb (200kN)
Cylinder bore: 11in (0.27m)
Cylinder stroke: 14in (0.35m)
Main generator type: Crompton
CG391A1
Aux generator type: Crompton
CAG193A1
Traction motor type: Crompton
C171C2
Gear ratio: 62:17
Fuel tank capacity: 750gal (3,410lit)
Cooling water capacity: 230gal
(1,046lit)
Lub oil capacity: 108gal (491lit)
Region of allocation: Southern
**Works responsible for classified
overhauls:** Eastleigh

Below:
*Class 33s are all allocated to the SR and are maintained at either Eastleigh or Hither
Green depots. Three sub-classes exist within Class 33: '33/0' standard locomotive,
'33/1' push-pull fitted locomotives, '33/2' narrow bodied locomotives for the Hastings
line. This view of No 33.064 at Ashford shows No 2 end, at the left between the bogies
is the battery box and on the right the fuel tank.* Colin J. Marsden

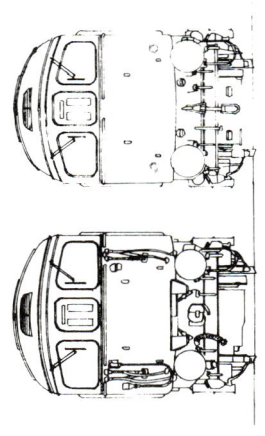

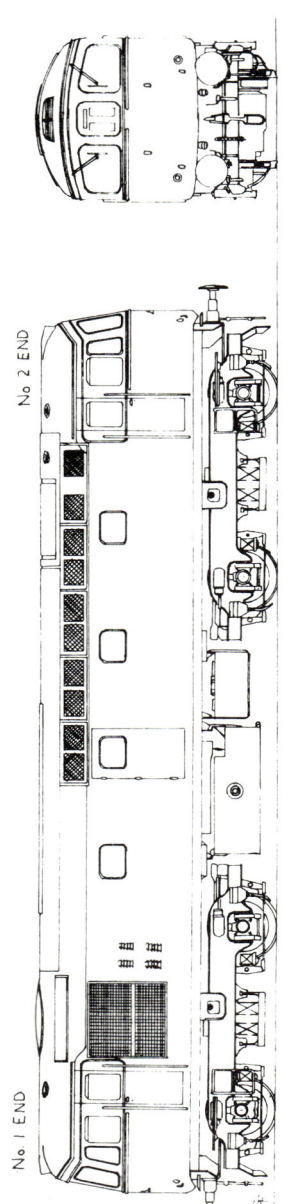

No 2 END

No I END

Above:
The side elevation of this drawing is representative of Class 33/0 locomotives only. There are several detail differences between this and the Class 33/1 and 33/2 sub-classes, and reference should be made to the illustrations to establish these. The three different front ends represent Classes 33/0, 33/1 and 33/2 respectively.

Left:
Front end detail for Class 33/0 and 33/2 (locomotive illustrated is 33/2.) 1. Control air pipe, 2. Electric train heat jumper socket, 3. Electric train heat jumper cable, 4. Main reservoir pipe, 5. Vacuum pipe, 6. Brake pipe, 7. Multiple unit (Blue Star) control jumper socket (cable kept in loco), 8. AWS receiving apparatus, 9. Rear marker light (not used and removed on some locomotives). Colin J. Marsden

Below:
Standard Class 33/0 viewed from No 2 end, with electrical equipment nearest the camera. The two sides of the Class 33 are almost identical except for small horizontal vents behind the radiator grille, there are four on one side but only two on the other. Another detail difference is the air filters at cant rail height, on one side there are 10 but the other side has 12. No 33.045 was photographed at Hither Green. Colin J. Marsden

Right:
Front end detail of Class 33/1 push-pull fitted locomotive. Note: during conversion work the redundant red tail indicators were removed. 1. Push-pull rubbing plate, 2. Dropable buck-eye coupling, 3. 27 wire push-pull jumper cable, 4. 27 wire push-pull jumper socket, 5. Waist height dual main reservoir/brake pipe cock, 6. Main reservoir pipe, 7. Air brake pipe, 8. Socket for lamp/bell attachment for working over Weymouth Quay line. All buffer beam fixtures are the same as on Class 33/0, 33/2 front illustration. Colin J. Marsden

Below:
The fleet of 19 Class 33/1 push-pull fitted locomotives were converted from standard locomotives during 1966/7 for use on the Waterloo-Weymouth line, where they were to take over from electric traction at Bournemouth, normally hauling TC stock. The locomotives are recognisable from standard examples by the additional air pipes and jumper cables carried at waist height, and the rubbing plate and buck-eye coupling at buffer beam level; all are allocated to Eastleigh. No 33.105 is seen at Clapham Junction coupled to a route learning saloon. Colin J. Marsden

Left:
The naming of selected examples of Class 33 commenced during 1979 when two were named after railway associated towns — Eastleigh and Ashford. These were followed by the two locomotives that hauled Earl Mountbatten of Burma's funeral train being named after him. The most recent naming of a Class 33 was No 33.025 Sultan, *after the naval establishment of the same name. It has become the norm for named Class 33s to be painted in slightly revised livery, with a grey roof, as depicted here on No 33.025 outside Stewarts Lane depot.* Colin J. Marsden

Left:
Detail of corporate identity style nameplate affixed to No 33.056 The Burma Star. *Under the nameplate is a non-standard Burma Star Coat of Arms, which looks especially attractive on the side of the Class 33 locomotive.* Colin J. Marsden

Below left:
The final 12 Class 33s built are classified as '33/2' and have a narrower body profile than Classes 33/0 and 33/1, thus enabling these locomotives to operate over the Hastings line where restricted clearances exist. Recognition of this sub-class is quite easy, as the body width continues from the frame width and does not protrude as on other sub-classes. The route indicator box is also slightly narrower. Another recognition factor is the two additional air vents (at cant rail height) on the Class 33/2 fleet; best identified if this and a view of a Class 33/0 are compared. Slow speed control equipment is fitted to all Class 33/2 locomotives, the equipment mounted on the inner wheel of the bogie at No 2 end. No 33.210 is viewed at Stewarts Lane depot from No 1 end. Colin J. Marsden

Above:
Class 33 Nos 33.001/003/004/008/013/015/022/027/029/030/032/033/037/039/044/046/049/051/054/056/058/060/201/202/206/212 are all fitted with three piece miniature snowploughs. These are normally painted black on this class of locomotive, but during the winter of 1982/3 several appeared in traffic painted in yellow. Although these are three piece ploughs the Class 33 fleet are proned to be in traffic with the centre plough removed, giving an unusual appearance. No 33.008 Eastleigh stands at Waterloo with a local service for Salisbury.   Colin J. Marsden

Below:
For several years it has been the wish of certain CM&EE staff to paint the Class 33s in a more distinctive livery and a start was made during the early 1980s when No 33.012 was given wrap round yellow ends, but alas this was removed when the locomotive passed through BREL Eastleigh works for classified overhaul. During 1982 another attempt to improve the appearance was made, when white window surrounds were added to some members of Class 33/1; this livery modification has now been applied to several locomotives and seems to have been accepted.   Colin J. Marsden

Class 37

Number series: 37.001-37.308
Former number: D6600-D6608, D6700-D6999
Built by: English Electric Vulcan Foundry, Robert Stephenson & Hawthorn Ltd
Introduced: 1960-1965
Type: Co-Co
Weight in running order: Various between 100-105 tonnes
Height: 12ft 9$^{1}/_{16}$in (3.89m)
Width: 8ft 10$^{3}/_{4}$in (2.70m)
Length: 61ft 6in (18.74m)
Min curve negotiable: 4 chains (80.46m)
Maximum speed: 90mph (145km/h)
Wheelbase: 50ft 8in (15.44m)
Bogie wheelbase: 13ft 6in (4.11m)
Bogie pivot centres: 37ft 2in (11.32m)
Wheel diameter — driving: 3ft 9in (1.14m)
Brake type: Vacuum, dual
Sanding equipment: Pneumatic
Heating type: Steam, Clayton RO 2000
Route availability: 5

Coupling restriction: Blue Star
Brake force: 50 tonnes
Engine type: English Electric 12CSVT
HP: 1,750hp (1,304kW)
Tractive effort: 55,500lb (247kN)
Cylinder bore: 10in (0.25m)
Cylinder stroke: 12in (0.30m)
Main generator type: English Electric 822/10G
Aux generator type: English Electric 911/5C
Traction motor type: English Electric 538/A
Gear ratio: 53:18
Fuel tank capacity: 890gal (4,046lit)
Cooling water capacity: 160gal (727lit)
Boiler water capacity: 800gal (3,637lit)
Lub oil capacity: 120gal (545lit)
Boiler fuel capacity: From main supply
Region of allocation: Eastern, Scottish, Western
Works responsible for classified overhauls: Crewe, Doncaster

Below:
One of the most successful Type 3 locomotives ever built is the Class 37, designed and built by English Electric. There are two different body designs within the class, the first 119 locomotives were built with central corridor connections and having their four position headcode box split each side of the gangway connection, while later locomotives have a solid central headcode box. Split box No 37.033 still retaining its front end doors, stands in the works yard at BREL Doncaster. Colin J. Marsden

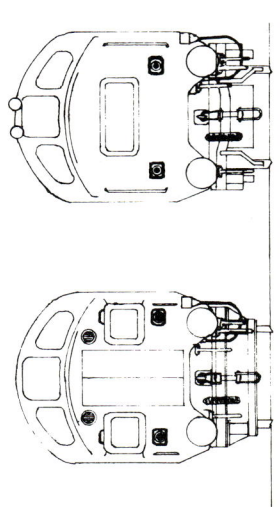

No 2 END

No I END

Above:
There are two distinct body designs in the Class 37 fleet. Locomotives Nos 37.001-119 are fitted with split route indicator boxes, formerly each side of a central gangway door, whilst the remainder of the fleet have solid central route indicator boxes. The front end valance behind the buffer beams are in the course of modification being straightened at buffer beam level. This side elevation is of a locomotive in the number range 37.001-119, with the two different front end designs both shown.

Left:
Front end of Class 37 fitted with split headcode boxes. Note: On locomotives after No 37.120, a solid central four position headcode box was fitted; this modification also enabled the warning horns to be repositioned on the cab roof. 1. Engine control air pipe, 2. Main reservoir air pipe, 3. Vacuum pipe, 4. Steam pipe, 5. Multiple unit (Blue Star) control jumper socket, 6. Multiple unit (Blue Star) control jumper cable, 7. Red tail indicator light, 8. Warning horns. This is a vacuum braked only locomotive. If dual brakes were fitted an air brake pipe would be positioned above the steam pipe.
Michael Collins

Centre left:
All locomotives had a valance around the buffers when built, but from the late 1970s these have been removed when locomotives passed through main works for classified attention. This modification is noticeable if this and the previous plate are compared. Split box No 37.067 with sealed up nose end doors, is viewed from No 1 end. On this example the outer mesh of the radiator grille has been removed, a feature that has only occurred in recent years. Colin J. Marsden

Bottom left:
Locomotives Nos 37.120-308 were built with one piece solid central headcode boxes and roof mounted warning horns. Of course, in recent years, headcode boxes have displayed only two white marker lights. Several locomotives not requiring the steam heating facility have had their boiler water tank (on underframe) converted to a second fuel tank, locomotives so treated are normally only recognisable by a stencilled note on the tank. No 37.193 in immaculate ex-works condition, is viewed from No 2 end.
Colin J. Marsden

Right:
A special modification was carried out to No 37.292 when it passed through works in 1981 — the uprating of the locomotive's power unit to develop 2,000hp; however from the outside there are no external differences. This locomotive is normally used in the Motherwell area working in multiple with another member of the class on heavy freight duties. Various modifications have been made to the radiator grilles of Class 37 locomotives. On some the external mesh has been completely removed, whilst others, as illustrated here, are fitted with a coarse mesh cover. This view shows No 37.292 while undergoing DM&EE testing at BREL Doncaster prior to return to traffic.   Colin J. Marsden

Right:
Some Class 37 locomotives have been given official names in recent years, of the corporate identity style. Five Scottish allocated locomotives are named after Lochs and these carry an additional side embellishment of a painted West Highland terrier dog under the nameplate, because of the locomotives' association with the West Highland line. The name and dog crest of No 37.081 Loch Long *is shown here.   Colin J. Marsden*

Bottom right:
The Class 37 fleet is allocated to Eastern, Western and Scottish Regions with the largest allocation being on the Eastern, followed by the Western and Scottish. However these versatile Type 3 locomotives often operate on to all regions of the BR network and are frequently used on passenger and freight duties. Snowplough fitted No 37.040 is seen passing Horbury wagon works, near Healey Mills, a stronghold for the class.
Colin J. Marsden

Class 40

Number series: 40.001-40.199*
Former number: D200-D399
Built by: English Electric Vulcan Foundry, Robert Stevenson & Hawthorn Ltd
Introduced: 1958-1962
Type: 1Co-Co1
Weight in running order: 133 tonnes
Height: 12ft 10in (3.91m)
Width: 9ft 0in (2.74m)
Length: 69ft 6in (21.18m)
Min curve negotiable: 4½ chains (90.52m)
Maximum speed: 90mph (145km/h)
Wheelbase: 61ft 3in (18.66m)
Bogie wheelbase: 21ft 6in (6.55m)
Bogie pivot centres: 34ft 4in (10.46m)
Wheel diameter — driving: 3ft 9in (1.14m)
Wheel diameter — pony: 3ft 0in (0.91m)
Brake type: Vacuum, dual
Sanding equipment: Pneumatic
Heating type: Steam — Stones OK4625 or Clayton RO2500
Route availability: 6
Coupling restriction: Blue Star (if fitted)

Brake force: 51 tonnes
Engine type: English Electric 16 SVT MKII
HP: 2,000hp (1,490kW)
Tractive effort: 52,000lb (231kN)
Cylinder bore: 10in (0.25m)
Cylinder stroke: 12in (0.30m)
Main generator type: English Electric EE 822 DC
Aux generator type: English Electric EE 911 DC
Traction motor type: English Electric EE 526/5D
Gear ratio: 61:19
Fuel tank capacity: 710gal (3,228lit)
Cooling water capacity: 200gal (909lit)
Boiler water capacity: 800gal (3,637lit)
Lub oil capacity: 140gal (636lit)
Boiler fuel capacity: 200gal (909lit)
Region of allocation: Eastern, Midland
Works responsible for classified overhauls: Crewe
* Many now withdrawn. Class scheduled for early withdrawal

Below:
The first large fleet of Type 4 locomotives ordered to replace steam traction during the 1950s was this fleet of English Electric locomotives, now classified as Class 40. A total of 200 was built but now under 60 remain, and the fleet is likely to be extinct by the end of 1984. Three different front end designs exist within the Class 40 build. The first 125 locomotives were built with nose end corridor connections and disc headcodes, as displayed here on now withdrawn No 40.007 at Tinsley, photographed from the No 1 end. Colin J. Marsden

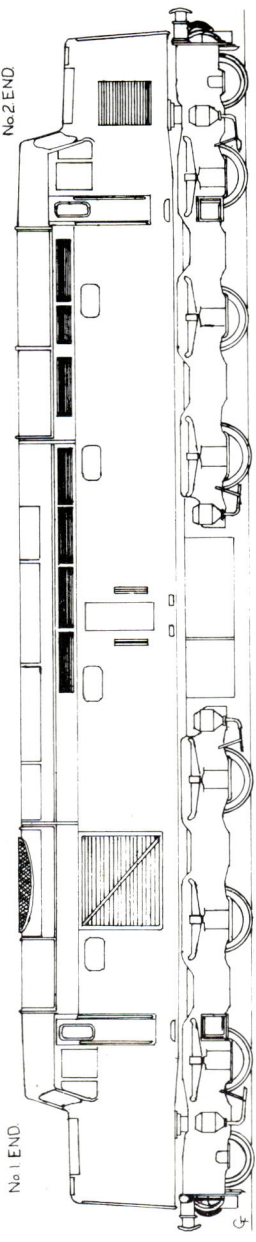

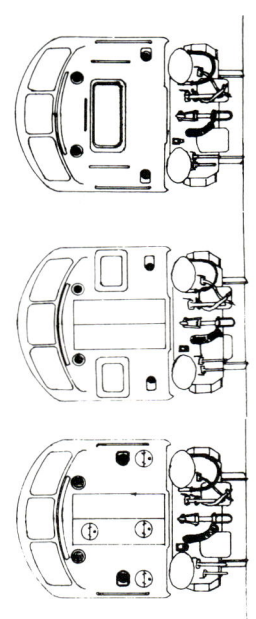

No.1 END.

No.2 END

Above:
Three different body styles exist within the rapidly diminishing Class 40 fleet. The first 125 locomotives were built with the disc headcode system; the next 20 locomotives Nos 40.125-144 had split headcode boxes, two digits each side of the nose end gangway door; and the remainder of the fleet Nos 40.145-199 were built with a one piece central four position headcode box. This side elevation drawing shows a disc headcode example, fitted with a boiler water tank. All three front end designs are illustrated. Some disc headcode locomotives have had these removed in recent years with just the marker lights remaining.

55

Above:
Front end layout of the two most numerous designs. Locomotives fitted with a split box headcode are basically the same as the disc fitted locomotive except, of course, that the discs and associated equipment are removed. On the left we see the original disc headcode fitted locomotive depicted by No 40.004, whilst on the right the final design of nose end displayed by No 40.157 can be seen. 1. Engine control air pipe, 2. Main reservoir pipe, 3. Vacuum pipe, 4. Air brake pipe (not fitted on vacuum only locomotives — now extinct), 5. Steam pipe, 6. Multiple unit (Blue Star) control jumper socket, 7. Multiple unit (Blue Star) control jumper cable. 8. Red tail indicator light, 9. Warning horns. Michael Collins/Colin J. Marsden

Below:
The revised solid headcode panel fitted to the final 55 locomotives, cleaned up the rather cluttered front end, but to many enthusiasts the disc headcoded locomotives are still preferred. In this view of No 40.178 hauling a Class 08 locomotive past Stainforth, we are looking at the No 2 end, in which the boiler is housed on steam heat fitted examples. The equipment between the bogies is a boiler water tank but on some non-heat fitted locomotives these have been removed. Colin J. Marsden

Right:

The small batch of locomotives Nos 40.125-40.144 were built with split headcode boxes, two positions each side of the central gangway. No 40.129 is seen here standing at Workington depot still sporting its nose end gangway doors, when photographed during early 1983. During re-design work to remove the disc headcode system, the red tail lights were fitted in a slightly lower position. Colin J. Marsden

Centre right:

All Class 40s were built with the Blue Star multiple-unit control system, however a number of locomotives have since had this removed when the equipment became faulty. Locomotives so treated can be recognised by the omission of the jumper cable and socket on the buffer beam, illustrated here on No 40.004 standing with a Class 25 at Carlisle. Ian Gould

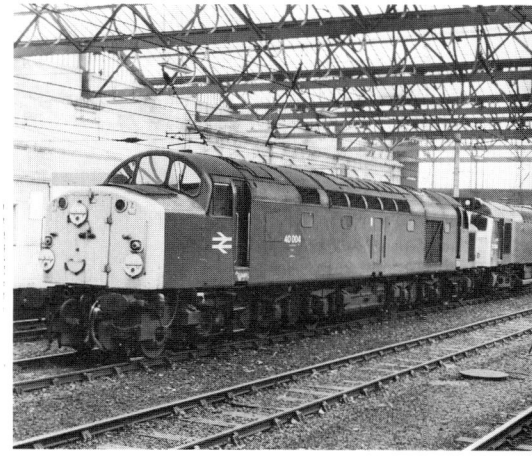

Bottom right:

The last surviving BR main line locomotive in green livery was No 40.106 and when it passed through works for a classified overhaul during the late 1970s much pressure was placed on management to retain this distinctive livery. Those wishes were honoured and No 40.106 returned to traffic to operate a number of special and regular trains painted in BR green with a full yellow end, until mid-1983 when it was withdrawn following a bogie frame fracture.
No 40.106 is photographed here near Colwyn Bay with a Bangor-Manchester Victoria service. No 40.122 formerly No D200 was returned to green livery in the summer of 1983 and used in normal traffic. Andrew Floyd

Class 45

Number series: 45.001-45.077, 45.101-45.150
Former number: D1-D137
Built by: BR at Derby and Crewe
Introduced: 1960-1961
Type: 1Co-Co1
Weight in running order: 136 tonnes
Height: 12ft 10⅛in (3.91m)
Width: 8ft 10⅝in (2.70m)
Length: 67ft 11in (20.70m)
Min curve negotiable: 5 chains (100.58m)
Maximum speed: 90mph (145km/h)
Wheelbase: 59ft 8in (18.18m)
Bogie wheelbase: 21ft 6in (6.55m)
Bogie pivot centres: 32ft 8in (9.95m)
Wheel diameter— driving: 3ft 9in (1.14m)
Wheel diameter — pony: 3ft 0in (0.91m)
Brake type: Dual
Sanding equipment: Pneumatic
Heating type: 45/0 — steam — Stones OK 4625
45/1 — electric — Index No 66

Route availability: 7
Brake force: 63 tonnes
Engine type: Sulzer 12LDA28B
HP: 2,500hp (1,862.5kW)
Tractive effort: 55,000lb (245kN)
Cylinder bore: 11in (0.27m)
Cylinder stroke: 14in (0.35m)
Main generator type: Crompton CG426A1
Aux generator type: Crompton CAG252A1
Traction motor type: Crompton C172A1
Gear ratio: 62:17
Fuel tank capacity: 790gal (3,591lit)
Cooling water capacity: 346gal (1,572lit)
Boiler water capacity (Class 45/0): 1,040gal (4,727lit)
Lub oil capacity: 190gal (864lit)
Boiler fuel capacity (Class 45/0): From main supply
Region of allocation: Eastern, Midland
Works responsible for classified overhauls: Crewe, Derby

Below:
Two distinctive types of Class 45 are in traffic, Class 45/0 — steam heat fitted, and Class 45/1 — electric heat fitted. Recognition is best achieved by reference to the front end to see if a steam heat pipe or an electric train heat jumper and socket are provided. Class 45/0 No 45.076 is illustrated here from the No 2 end, which houses the train heating boiler. Colin J. Marsden

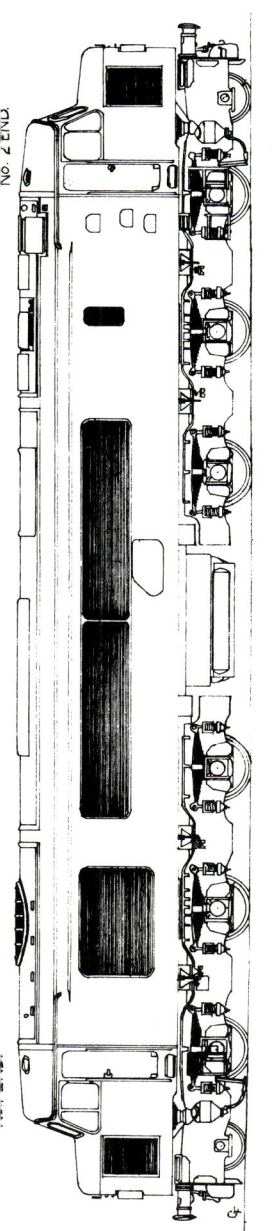

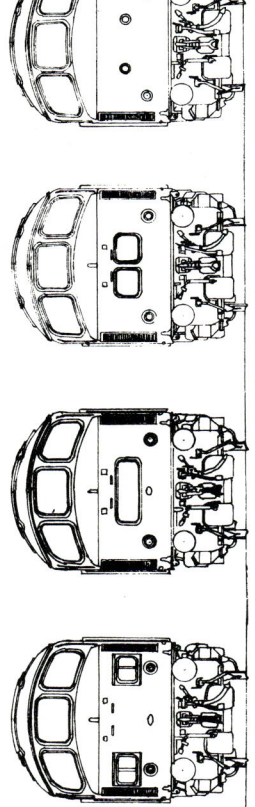

Above:
Two distinct types of Class 45 are in service — 45/0 locomotives are fitted with steam heat equipment, and 45/1 have the electric train heat system. This side elevation represents a Class 45/0. Four different front ends are shown: When built Nos D11-D31 and D68-D107 were fitted with split four position headcode boxes, two each side of a central gangway position. The remainder of the fleet were either fitted with a two-piece or solid central four position headcode. Following a decision to dispense with headcodes during the 1970s, the Class 45s had their front ends remodelled to accommodate two fixed beam headlights in the former headcode position.

Above:
Front end detail of both types of Class 45 locomotive. On the left a Class 45/0 fitted with steam heating, and on the right a Class 45/1 fitted with electric train heating. 1. Main reservoir pipe, 2. Air brake pipe, 3. Vacuum pipe, 4. Steam pipe, 5. Electric train heat jumper socket, 6. Electric train heat jumper cable, 7. Red tail indicator light, 8. Headlamp (sealed beam type). Michael Collins/Colin J. Marsden

Below:
View of Class 45/1 taken from No 1 end, which houses the radiator and collant group, identifiable by the large square grille on the body side. When the Class 45 fleet were built three different front end designs were used. (a) Split headcode boxes either side of a centre gangway position, (b) split headcode box mounted central on the nose end, (c) one piece central headcode. Following the decision to discontinue the four character headcode system, as the 'Peak' class locomotives passed through works the train identification system was replaced by two fixed beam headlights, mounted centrally on a plain front end. No 45.137 departs from Paignton with the 16.40 service to Waterloo on 5 September 1982. Colin J. Marsden

Right:
When originally built locomotives Nos D32-D67, D108-D137 were fitted with central split headcode boxes, however most of these have now been removed in favour of the two fixed beam lights. This view of steam heat fitted No 45.036 shows the locomotive from the No 1 end. The equipment between the bogies consists of two battery boxes (upper) and a boiler water tank (lower). On electric train heat fitted examples the boiler tank is filled with ballast weight.
Colin J. Marsden

Centre right:
The original Class 44 locomotives (now withdrawn) were all named after mountain peaks which gave the 'Peak' title to the class, and subsequent builds of the same design. The naming policy was continued on selected members of the Class 45 fleet but this time Regimental names being chosen; naming took place in the 1960s. The cast nameplate and regimental crest of No 45.006 The Honourable Artillery Company *is shown here.*
Steve Montgomery

Bottom right:
The Class 45 allocation is divided between Midland and Eastern regions, with all electric train heat fitted examples being allocated to Toton (TO), and the Class 45/0 members at either Toton (TO) or Tinsley (TI). Locomotives are regularly diagrammed to operate on LMR, ER and WR main line passenger and freight traffic and make occasional trips to the Scottish and Southern Regions. Here No 45.033 stands at Newcastle station at the head of the 20.00 travelling Post Office train to Bristol. Colin J. Marsden

Class 46

Number series: 46.001-46.056*
Former number: D138-D193
Built by: BR Derby
Introduced: From 1961
Type: 1Co-Co1
Weight in running order: 138tonnes
Height: 12ft 10⅛in (3.91m)
Width: 8ft 10⅛in (2.70m)
Length: 67ft 11in (20.70m)
Min curve negotiable: 5 chains (100.58m)
Maximum speed: 90mph (145km/h)
Wheelbase: 59ft 8in (18.18m)
Bogie wheelbase: 21ft 6in (6.55m)
Bogie pivot centres: 32ft 8in (9.95m)
Wheel diameter — driving: 3ft 9in (1.14m)
Wheel diameter — pony: 3ft 0in (0.91m)
Brake type: Dual
Sanding equipment: Pneumatic
Heating type: Steam — Spanner Mk 3 or Stones OK4625

Route availability: 7
Brake force: 63 tonnes
Engine type: Sulzer 12LDA28B
HP: 2,500hp (1,862.5kW)
Tractive effort: 55,000lb (245kN)
Cylinder bore: 11in (0.27m)
Cylinder stroke: 14in (0.35m)
Main generator type: Brush TG160-60
Aux generator type: Brush TG69-28
Traction motor type: Brush TM73-68
Gear ratio: 62:19
Fuel tank capacity: 790gal (3,591lit)
Cooling water capacity: 346gal (1,572lit)
Boiler water capacity: 1,040gal (4,727lit)
Lub oil capacity: 190gal (864lit)
Boiler fuel capacity: From main supply
Region of allocation: Eastern
Works responsible for classified overhauls: Derby
* Many now withdrawn. Class scheduled for early withdrawal.

Below:
The body design of the Class 46 is almost identical to a Class 45 except that on some locomotives the grilles by the boiler compartment may be left uncovered. When built Class 46s were either fitted with a two piece or solid central headcode box. In recent years, in common with the Class 45, front ends have been rebuilt to accommodate two fixed beam headlights.

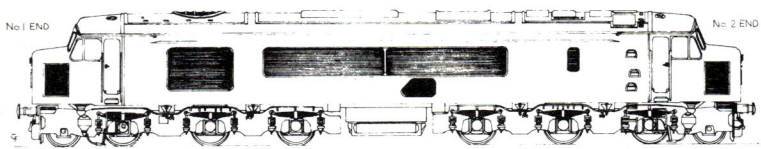

Above:
Recognition between members of Class 45/0 and Class 46 is by far the hardest of the current classes operating on the BR network, and is best achieved by reference to the number, although if the battery box covers are visible it will be seen that the Class 46 ones are plain whereas the Class 45s sport an 'X' shaped pattern. Although the appearance of the locomotives is the same, the internal equipment differs — Class 46s are fitted with a Brush electrical system in place of Crompton Parkinson equipment on the Class 45s. No 46.046, viewed from the No 1 end, approaches Totnes with a westbound cement during 1980. Colin J. Marsden

Below:
The Class 46 fleet was deemed as non-standard during the late 1970s and large inroads were made to the fleet with the result that it is unlikely that any member will still be in operation after the end of 1984. All locomotives are allocated to Gateshead (GD) (Newcastle) and can usually be observed on inter-regional services sometimes as far afield as into Cornwall. One member of the fleet is named, No 46.026 Leicestershire and Derbyshire Yeomanry, *making it easily recognisable. The illustration shows No 46.034 in undercoat at Derby works during 1978. This locomotive has now been withdrawn.* Colin J. Marsden

Class 47

	47/0	47/3	47/4	47/7	47/9
Sub Class:					
Number series:	47.001-47.299	47.301-47.381	47.401-47.637	47.701-47.712	47.901
Former number:	D1521-D1998 (at random)	D1782-D1900	D1100-D1957 (at random)	Class 47/4 (at random)	47.046 (D1628)
Built by:	BR Crewe, Brush Ltd	BR Crewe, Brush Ltd	BR Crewe, Brush Ltd	BR Crewe, Brush Ltd	BR Crewe
Introduced:	1962-1965	1962-1965	1962-1965	1962-1965	1964
Type:	Co-Co	Co-Co	Co-Co	Co-Co	Co-Co
Weight in running order:	109-117 tonnes	111 tonnes	118-123 tonnes	120 tonnes	118 tonnes
Height:	12ft 9⅞in (3.89m)	12ft 9⅞in (3.89m)	12ft 9⅞in (3.89m)	12ft 9⅞in (3.89m)	12ft 9⅞in (3.89m)
Width:	9ft 2in (2.79m)	9ft 2in (2.79m)	9ft 2in (2.79m)	9ft 2in (2.79m)	9ft 2in (2.79m)
Length:	63ft 7in (19.38m)	63ft 7in (19.38m)	63ft 7in (19.38m)	63ft 7in (19.38m)	63ft 7in (19.38m)
Min curve negotiable:	4 chains (80.46m)	4 chains (80.46m)	4 chains (80.46m)	4 chains (80.46m)	4 chains (80.46m)
Maximum speed:	95mph (153km/h)	95mph (153km/h)	95mph (153km/h)	95mph (153km/h)	80mph (129km/h)
Wheelbase:	51ft 6in (15.69m)	51ft 6in (15.69m)	51ft 6in (15.69m)	51ft 6in (15.69m)	51ft 6in (15.69m)
Bogie wheelbase:	14ft 6in (4.41m)	14ft 6in (4.41m)	14ft 6in (4.41m)	14ft 6in (4.41m)	14ft 6in (4.41m)
Bogie pivot centres:	37ft 0in (11.27m)	37ft 0in (11.27m)	37ft 0in (11.27m)	37ft 0in (11.27m)	37ft 0in (11.27m)
Wheel diameter — driving:	3ft 9in (1.14m)	3ft 9in (1.14m)	3ft 9in (1.14m)	3ft 9in (1.14m)	3ft 9in (1.14m)
Brake type:	Dual	Dual	Dual/electric	Dual	Air
Heating type:	Steam*	Not fitted	Dual	Electric	Not fitted
Route availability:	6	6	6	6	6
Brake force:	60 tonnes	60 tonnes	60 tonnes	60 tonnes	60 tonnes
Engine type:	Sulzer 12LDA28C	Sulzer 12LDA28C	Sulzer 12LDA28C	Sulzer 12LDA28C	Ruston Paxman 12RK3CT
HP:	2,580hp (1,922kW)	2,580hp (1,922kW)	2,580hp (1,922kW)	2,580hp (1,922kW)	3,300hp (2,455kW)
Tractive effort:	60,000lb (267kN)	60,000lb (267kN)	60,000lb‡ (267kN)	60,000lb (267kN)	57,325lb (255kN)
Cylinder bore:	11in (0.27m)	11in (0.27m)	11in (0.27m)	11in (0.27m)	10in (0.25m)
Cylinder stroke:	14in (0.35in)	14in (0.35in)	14in (0.35in)	14in (0.35in)	12in (0.30m)
Main generator type:	Brush TG160.60 or TG172.50	Brush TG160.60 or TG172.50	Brush TG160.60 or TG172.50	Brush TG160.60 or TG172.50	Brush BA 1101A†
Aux generator type:	Brush TG69.20 or TG69.28	Brush TG69.20 or TG69.28	Brush TG69.20 or TG69.28	Brush TG69.20 or TG69.28	Brush BAA 602A/ BAE503†
Traction motor type:	Brush TM64.68	Brush TM64.68	Brush TM64.68	Brush TM64.68	Brush TM73.62
Gear ratio:	66:17	66:17	66:17	66:17	66:17
Fuel tank capacity:	765gal (3,477lit)	765gal (3,477lit)	765gal (3,477lit)	765gal (3,477lit)	765gal (3,477lit)
Cooling water capacity:	300gal (1,364lit)	300gal (1,364lit)	300gal (1,364lit)	300gal (1,364lit)	308gal (1,400lit)
Boiler water capacity:	1,250gal (5,683lit)	Not fitted	1,250gal (5,683lit)	Not fitted	Not fitted
Lub oil capacity:	190gal (864lit)	190gal (864lit)	190gal (864lit)	190gal (864lit)	120gal (545lit)

Works responsible for classified overhauls: Crewe   Crewe   Crewe   Crewe   Crewe   Crewe

† alternator
* if fitted
‡ 47.401-420 55,000lb (245kN)

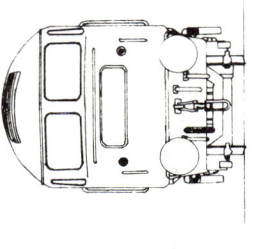

Note: The most numerous class of main line locomotive now in traffic is the BR/Brush Type 4, Class 47, and there are currently five sub-classes in operation.

1. '47/0' including locomotive numbers starting '47/1' and '47/2' — basic locomotive either fitted for steam heat or with the provision for steam heat to be fitted;

2. '47/3' — locomotives not fitted with any provision for train heat;

3. '47/4' including numbers starting in the 47.5 and 47/6 range — locomotives fitted with electric or dual train heating facilities;

4. '47/7' — electric heated locomotives fitted for push-pull (lighting wire) operation;

5. '47/9' — experimental locomotive fitted with Class 58 power unit for evaluation.

Below:
Various body modifications exist within the substantial Class 47 fleet. The drawing here represents a standard Class 47/0 locomotive, retaining the steam heating boiler water tanks on the underframe. Reference to the illustrations will show detail differences in the various sub-classes.

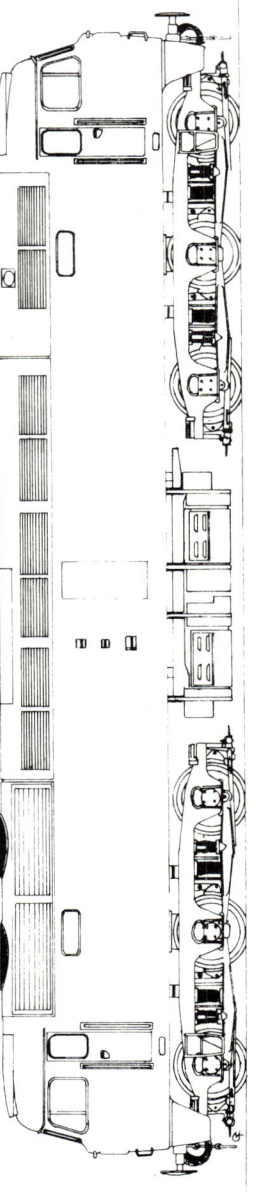

N° 2 END

N° 1 END.

Front end variations for Class 47s. Top left — Class 47/0, Top right — Class 47/3, Bottom left— Class 47/4, Bottom right — Class 47/7. 1. Main reservoir pipe, 2. Brake pipe, 3. Vacuum pipe, 4. Steam pipe, 5. Electric train heating jumper cable, 6. Electric train heating jumper socket, 7. Push-pull control jumper (train lighting system), 8. Headlight/sealed beam markers (different designs are in existence), 9. Red rear marker light.

Colin J. Marsden, (Bottom right) David Nicholas

Above:
This semi-roof view of a Class 47/0 locomotive taken from the No 1 end, shows where the radiator and coolant group are located. The removable roof sections are clearly visible in this view. The light coloured fibreglass sections cover the engine and generator compartment, and the two centre sections open out to give access to the top of the power unit. If a larger opening is required the complete roof section can be removed. No 47.032 is seen here at Par.   Colin J. Marsden

Below:
Both sides of a Class 47 are identical with two oblong windows giving a small amount of light to the radiator and boiler compartments. The locomotive illustrated here is shown from the No 2 end, which houses the train heating boiler (if fitted) or a ballast block on no heat examples. Between the bogies two battery boxes are normally situated with a boiler water tank in between, but in recent years the boiler water tank has been removed from a number of no-heat or electric heat locomotives and replaced by a space frame. No 47.212 is seen here at York.   Colin J. Marsden

Above:
The removal of the boiler water tank from non-heat fitted and electric heat fitted locomotives has given some locomotives an odd external appearance, however a spacing frame has been fitted and some underslung pipework still remains. Mid-way along the bodyside, on both sides of the locomotive, is a door operable only from the inside of the engine compartment, this is purely a service door giving additional access to the power unit. No 47.238, a non-heat example, is seen here at Crewe.
Barry J. Nicolle

Below:
Since the abolition of the four position headcode system during the mid-1970s and the requirement for two white lights to be displayed on the nose end of trains, various modifications of marker light have been fitted to the Class 47 fleet. Most locomotives had their headcode box blacked out with two white circles left clear, others had the headcode box plated and two white grommeted opaque glasses fitted, and some had fixed beam headlights fitted, as was the case of No 47.249 illustrated here at Bristol Bath Road. Colin J. Marsden

Above:
Eighty-one members of the Class 47 fleet were constructed with no facility for either steam or electric train heating and under the TOPS renumbering and classification system these locomotives became Class 47/3. The only external difference between these and the '47/0s' is the omission of the steam heat pipe from the buffer beam, and recognition of this sub-class is best achieved by reference to the running number which will be between 47.301-381. No 47.314 is seen here at Nuneaton. Colin J. Marsden

Below:
The first 20 members of the electric train heat sub-class Nos 47.401-420, are recognisable from the remainder of the type by having their ETH jumpers mounted on the buffer beam, rather than on the nose end. The majority of these first 20 locomotives are fitted with dual heating, identifiable by the presence of both electric heat jumpers and a steam heat pipe on the buffer beam. All these examples are allocated to Gateshead (GD) depot but can be found operating all over the country. No 47.403 departs from St Austell with a Penzance bound train. This recognition factor has now been lost as recent ETH conversions have had the jumper cables fitted in the buffer beam. Colin J. Marsden

Above:
Some strange and non-standard livery modifications exist within the Class 47 fleet. Several locomotives, especially those allocated to South Wales, have the last three numerals of their running number stencilled below the former route indicator box, and this unique example, apparently No 47.242 of CF, not only has 242 on the front but also sports a black cab roof and black cab window surrounds. Brian Morrison

Below:
During the 1970s two Class 47s Nos 47.277/373 were fitted with yellow roof beacons due to a remote slow speed facility being installed for use on certain colliery lines on ER. It is understood that these lights are to be removed as locomotives pass through works on classified overhaul. The light is clearly visible on No 47.277 as it leads Class 40 No 40.015 out of Dringhouses yard, York on 9 September 1981. Colin J. Marsden

Above:
Sealed beam quartz headlights were fitted to a number of Class 47 locomotives to evaluate the effect on train crews and staff working about the tracks, however the majority have now been removed and a blanking plate fitted in its place. In this view of No 47.523 the lamp can be seen under the driver's side red tail lamp. Barry J. Nicolle

Below:
Another fitment during the 1970s to Class 47s Nos 47.370/379 was a novel system of push-pull operation using waist level mounted train lighting control jumpers. This proved to be rarely used and was removed from both locomotives in the early 1980s when passing through main works for classified overhaul. However No 47.370 retains the head pockets on the nose end, under the former route panel, thus giving a recognition factor to this locomotive. No 47.370 is seen at Langley oil terminal. Michael Collins

Above:
*A number of Scottish Region Class 47s with electric train heating have been
fitted with miniature snowploughs in recent years. However the fitting of these basic
items was not as straight forward as it might have first seemed, for the ETH jumpers
and socket were behind the plough fitting and had to be repositioned. This can be seen
in this view of No 47.550*   Derek Porter

Below:
*The most recent sub-class of Class 47 to be introduced is the 12 members of '47/7',
these are electric train heat fitted examples with push-pull equipment by means of train
lighting cables. These locomotives are immediately recognisable by the additional
cables on the front end at waist height. All locomotives are allocated to HA and used in
conjunction with push-pull fitted stock on the Edinburgh-Glasgow route and other
selected routes in southern Scotland. No 47.701* St Andrew *stands inside its home
depot under repair.*   Ian Gould

Above:
Converted to operate with the fleet of push-pull fitted Class 47/7 locomotives were 10 DBSO (Driving Brake Second Open) coaches rebuilt from Mk 2f BSO vehicles. During the conversion work at BREL Glasgow driving controls and a small cab were fitted into part of the former luggage van. Electric headlight, marker and tail lights were also provided as well as an emergency nose end corridor door, (not normally used). Each vehicle carries a set number in the 6xx range under the driving window. Set 606, propelled by a Class 47/7 locomotive approaches Larbert Junction with the 10.28 Perth-Glasgow on 26 August 1982.   Kim Fullbrook

Below:
The last two members of Class 47/7 Nos 47.711/712 were outshopped during 1981 in revised livery, sporting wrap round yellow ends, black window surrounds, grey roof, large numbers and BR logo, a livery that has enhanced the Class 47 appearance. No 47.711 Greyfriars Bobby *is seen outside Haymarket shed in Edinburgh, photographed from the No 1 end.*   John Tuffs

Left:
Class 47/0 No 47.046 suffered serious collision damage during the 1970s and was taken to BREL Crewe works for major rebuilding. Whilst there awaiting repairs a test bed was required to evaluate Class 56 equipment. No 47.046 was selected for this task and was completely redesigned internally to take a Class 56 power unit and other equipment. The locomotive returned to the main line for trials carrying No 47.601. Minor exterior alterations were also carried out including the filling in of one side window at No 2 end, fitting a quartz headlight and sand laying system, but most importantly the locomotive was fitted for train air brake operation only. After the satisfactory evaluation tests were completed the locomotive returned to Crewe works and was again rebuilt, this time with equipment intended for Class 58 freight locomotives then being developed. The locomotive emerged during late 1980 to take up operation firstly on ER and then on the WR, always hauling heavy freight trains. After rebuilding as the Class 58 test bed the locomotive was again renumbered to 47.901 and was photographed here at Westbury.
Colin J. Marsden

Below:
Nameplates were fixed to selected WR allocated Class 47s during the 1960s, of the distinctive Western style. No further naming took place until the late 1970s when the policy was revived with all subsequent plates being of corporate identity style. In the upper illustration the nameplate of No 47.088 Samson is shown, with the lower view depicting the modern style nameplate carried by No 47.703 Saint Mungo.
Both Barry J. Nicolle

Above:
The Class 47 fleet is allocated to all regions of BR except the Southern, but this region sees considerable use of the class as drivers from all three Southern divisions are trained on their operation, and the locomotives are regularly diagrammed into the region on both passenger and freight trains. Steam heat fitted No 47.171 with number stencilled on the nose end, passes West Ealing with a rake of Mk 1 coaches whilst working an Oxford-Paddington local service.
Colin J. Marsden

Right:
A recent modification to a number of Class 47s is the addition of an off centre fixed beam headlight, under the former route indicator box. This fitting is shown here on No 47.308.
Colin J. Marsden

Right:
The number of Class 47 main line passenger duties has diminished in recent years with the full introduction of IC125 passenger services. This was particularly noticeable when the North East-South West arterial route was changed over during 1982. Electric train heat fitted No 47.578 stands at Derby with a rake of Mk 2 coaches while forming a Newcastle-Cardiff service early in 1982.
Colin J. Marsden

Class 50

Number series: 50.001-50.050
Former number: D400-D449
Built by: English Electric at Vulcan Foundry
Introduced: 1967-1968
Type: Co-Co
Weight in running order: 115 tonnes
Height: 12ft 11¾in (3.95m)
Width: 9ft 1¼in (2.77m)
Length: 68ft 6in (20.87m)
Min curve negotiable: 4 chains (80.46m)
Maximum speed: 95mph (153km/h)
Wheelbase: 56ft 2in (17.11m)
Bogie wheelbase: 13ft 6in (4.11m)
Bogie pivot centres: 42ft 8in (13.00m)
Wheel diameter — driving: 3ft 7in (1.09m)
Brake type: Dual
Heating type: Electric — Index No 61
Route availability: 6

Coupling restriction: Orange Square
Brake force: 59 tonnes
Engine type: English Electric 16CSVT
HP: 2,700hp (2,049kW)
Tractive effort: 48,500lb (216kN)
Cylinder bore: 10in (0.25m)
Cylinder stroke: 12in (0.30m)
Main generator type: English Electric 840/4B
Aux generator type: English Electric 911/5C
Traction motor type: English Electric 538/5A
Gear ratio: 53:18
Fuel tank capacity: 1,055gal (4,796lit)
Cooling water capacity: 280gal (1,272.8lit)
Lub oil capacity: 130gal (591lit)
Region of allocation: Western
Works responsible for classified overhauls: Doncaster

Below:
Probably the most popular class of main line locomotive currently in operation is this fleet of 50 Class 50s. Initially the locomotives were built during 1967/8 for use on the LMR, being owned by English Electric Leasings, a subsidiary company of the builders. Following the full electrification of the Euston-Glasgow route during the mid-1970s, the locomotives were sold to BR and transferred to the WR to replace the Class 52 'Western' diesel-hydraulic locomotives. Due to the high failure rate of the locomotives and their general condition, a refurbishment programme to the complete class was undertaken during the late 1970s and early 1980s. After the first seven locomotives had been refurbished a change of livery took place with wrap round yellow ends, black window surrounds, grey roofs, large numbers and BR logo. No 50.016 Barham *is illustrated here at BREL Doncaster.* Colin J. Marsden

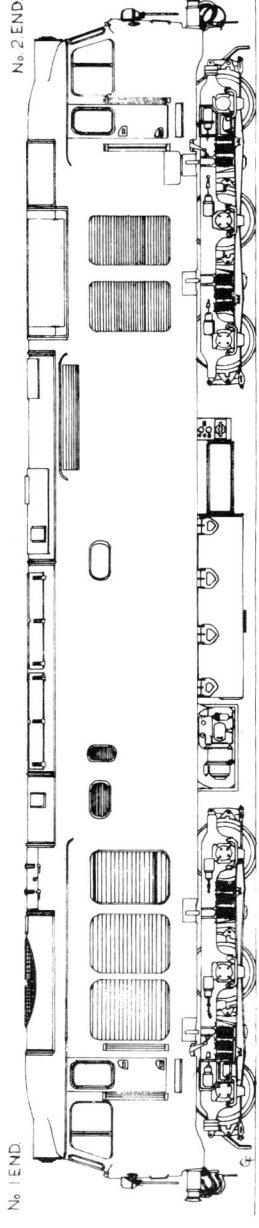

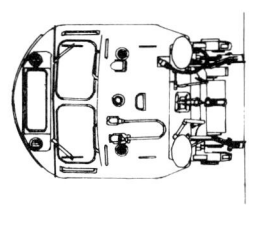

No. 1 END

No. 2 END

Above:
This drawing is representative of the complete fleet and shows a locomotive in refurbished condition with plated roof section above side air louvres, nose end fixed beam headlight and plated over sandboxes. (Some early refurbished examples in standard livery, may still have some sandbox fillers uncovered.)

Left:
*Class 50 front end layout:
1. Engine control air pipe, 2. Main reservoir pipe, 3. Air brake pipe, 4. Vacuum pipe, 5. Electric train heating jumper socket, 6. Electric train heating jumper cable, 7. Multiple-unit (Orange Square) jumper cable, 7A. Multiple-unit (Orange Square) jumper cable dummy socket (jumper housed here when not in use), 8. Multiple-unit (Orange Square) jumper socket, 9. Red tail light, 10. Headlight, 11. Front marker light, 12. Warning horns.*
Colin J. Marsden

Below:
View of refurbished Class 50 from No 1 end, where the radiator and coolant groups are housed. The two sides of the Class 50 are different, with on one side the main air filtration grilles at No 2 end. Between the bogies is housed the fuel tank capable of carrying 1,055gal of fuel enabling the locomotive to have nearly a 1,000 mile operating range. Also mounted on the underframe, in front of the fuel tank in this view is an air compressor. No 50.010 Monarch stands outside Laira depot (LA).
Colin J. Marsden

Right:
A Class 50 from No 2 end, with air filtration equipment nearest the camera. If this and the previous plate are compared it will be noted that only one window exists on this side, whereas the other has two. The equipment visible between the bogies on this side consists of air compressor (far end), fuel tank (middle), and batteries and battery isolating switch (near). No 50.035 Ark Royal *is seen outside Old Oak Common.*
Colin J. Marsden

Centre right:
When the first seven Class 50 locomotives passed through BREL Doncaster works for general/ refurbish overhaul, they were outshopped in standard rail blue livery and the only recognition factor between these and unrefurbished examples was the addition of the headlight on the nose end, the filling in of the lower roof section above the air filtration equipment, and the plating over of some sand box fillers. No 50.017 Royal Oak *refurbished in old livery, stands outside Old Oak Common depot during October 1982. The first seven refurbished locomotives will be passing through works during 1984 and will emerge in revised livery.* Michael Collins

Left:
Close up of cab No 2 end on refurbished locomotive, showing the former lower roof area above the air filtration grilles which has been built up to normal roof line profile. It will be noticed that the front sandbox has not been plated on this locomotive, a requirement of the refurbishing programme. In early 1984 it was announced that several Class 50s would be repainted in GWR green livery and renamed, the first to be done was 50.007 Sir Edward Elgar.
Colin J. Marsden

Above: *Class 50 in unrefurbished condition, from No 2 end. The four sandbox filling ports can be seen on the side. When refurbished one side window on both sides was replaced by a grille to improve engine room ventilation. No 50.028* Tiger *still sporting black route indicator panel with two white cut-outs for front indicators, stands at Penzance.* Colin J. Marsden

Left:
A naming policy for the Class 50 fleet commenced during 1978 with the allocation of warship names. Plates were fixed during 1978/9 without undue attention, but subsequently since 1979 twinning ceremonies have taken place with various Royal Naval Establishments bearing the same name, with the naval coat of arms being applied above the nameplate. In the upper view the name and ship's crest of No 50.025 Invincible *is shown, whilst in the lower plate the rather tatty name of No 50.015* Valiant *is illustrated.*
Both Colin J. Marsden

Above:
All 50 members of the Class 50 fleet are allocated to the Western Region at either Plymouth Laira (LA) or Old Oak Common (OC) depots, from where they operate to various points on the WR, excluding Wales, and to a number of locations outside the region such as Birmingham, Temple Mills and the Southern Region. No 50.045 Achilles *approaches Totnes with a Plymouth-Birmingham train during the late summer of 1981.* Colin J. Marsden

Below:
One of the main strongholds for the Class 50 fleet on passenger duties, is the Waterloo-Exeter route. Laira depot normally provides the power for this service but it is not unusual for OC allocated machines to be seen. No 50.038 Formidable *hurries the 11.10 Waterloo-Exeter around the curve at Clapham Junction on 13 August 1981.* Colin J. Marsden

Class 56

Number series: 56.001-56.135
Built by: Electroputere at Craiova in Romania, BREL Doncaster, BREL Crewe
Introduced: 1976-1984
Type: Co-Co
Weight in running order: 125 tonnes
Height: 13ft 0in (3.96m)
Width: 9ft 2in (2.79m)
Length: 63ft 6in (19.35m)
Min curve negotiable: 4 chains (70.40m)
Maximum speed: 80mph (129km/h)
Wheelbase: 47ft 10in (14.58m)
Bogie wheelbase: 13ft 5⅞in (4.10m)
Bogie pivot centres: 37ft 8in (11.48m)
Wheel diameter — driving: 3ft 9in (1.14m)
Brake type: Air
Sanding equipment: Pneumatic
Route availability: 7

Coupling restriction: Red Diamond
Brake force: 60 tonnes
Engine type: Ruston-Paxman 16RK3CT
HP: 3,250hp (2,420kW)
Tractive effort: 60,750lb (270kN)
Cylinder bore: 10in (0.25m)
Cylinder stroke: 12in (0.30m)
Main alternator type: Brush BA1101A
Aux alternator type: Brush BAA602A/ BAE503
Traction motor type: Brush TM73-62
Gear ratio: 63:16
Fuel tank capacity: 1,150gal (5,228lit)
Cooling water capacity: 308gal (1,400lit)
Lub oil capacity: 120gal (545lit)
Region of allocation: Eastern, Midland, Western
Works responsible for classified overhauls: Doncaster

Below:
The first new main line diesel locomotives to be ordered since the mid-1960s was the Class 56 heavy freight locomotives during the mid-1970s. Due to production timescales being impracticable in British workshops, Brush Traction Ltd was awarded the contract to build 30 Type 5 locomotives at their associated works of Electropute at Craiova in Romania. The completed locomotives were shipped to England via the Harwich train ferry. The building of subsequent orders for Class 56 locomotives took place at BR Doncaster and Crewe workshops culminating in 135 locomotives altogether. Detail differences do exist between Romanian and British builds. Romanian No 56.012 stands outside Knottingley depot. Colin J. Marsden

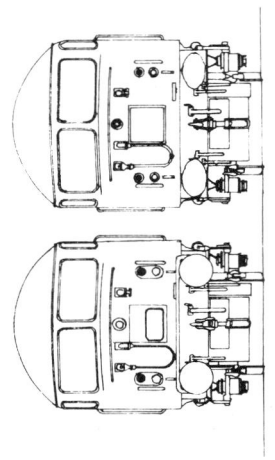

N° 1 END.

N° 2 END

Above:
Various detail differences exist within the Class 56 fleet, mainly involving front end arrangement and cab window detail. Both body sides are identical. Two front ends are shown — on the left is the original design applied to Nos 56.001–055, and on the right is the front detail on Nos 56.056–135. Some of the early designed locomotives may be outshopped with the later cab arrangement following collision damage repairs. Round or oval buffers are carried on either front end.

Left:
Class 56 front end detail; this style was applied to the original 30 Romanian locomotives but since then various modifications have occurred including different horn grilles, headlight, marker/tail lights and buffer beam. However all equipment is carried in the same place. 1. Engine control air pipe, 2. Main reservoir pipe, 3. Air brake pipe, 4. Multiple-Unit (Red Diamond) control jumper, 5. Multiple-unit (Red Diamond) control jumper socket, 6. Red tail indicator light, 7. White frontal marker light, 8. Fixed beam headlight, 9. Warning horns (under grille). Colin J. Marsden

Below:
Recognition of Romanian and British built examples is best achieved by reference to the cab side window area. On Romanian engines the two side windows are of two piece construction with the front portion mounted in a rubber grommet, whilst all British built locomotives have the two windows mounted in a common frame with a dividing column. Door windows on Romanian examples are also mounted in rubber grommets whereas British locomotives are fixed in an aluminium frame. On the left is Romanian locomotive No 56.006 while on the right is Doncaster built No 56.079. David Nicholas

Above:
Many frontal differences exist within the Class 56 fleet, and many of these alterations such as round or oval buffers, are not constant for a particular batch of locomotives. It has been observed that one locomotive has round buffers at one end and oval at the other! Viewed from No 2 end, No 56.080 stands with two other members of the class at Sunderland depot.
Colin J. Marsden

Below:
The recognition of No 1 and No 2 end of a Class 56 locomotive is not difficult, as the radiator and coolant group are situated at No 1 end and identifiable by the two large rectangular grilles on the body side. Equipment between the bogies consists of battery box, air compressor, with the fuel tank behind. No 56.004 stands on Doncaster depot.
Colin J. Marsden

Below:
The first main line locomotive to emerge in revised 'Railfreight' livery was Class 56 No 56.036, repainted by the workshop at Stratford (London) during the late 1970s. When the locomotive first appeared it caused considerable comment with 18in high running numbers, a full height BR logo, wrap round yellow ends, black window surrounds and a grey roof, however this livery was subsequently adopted as the norm for the class. No 56.036 is seen basking in the sun and snow in the works yard at Doncaster during early 1982.
Colin J. Marsden

Above:
Locomotives constructed after No 56.084 which emerged from BREL Doncaster from October 1980 were all painted in 'Railfreight' livery based on No 56.036. The livery has now been widely accepted and surprisingly suits the Class 56 design, giving a far more pleasing appearance than the original colour scheme. Although original liveried Class 56s are now passing through works for classified attention, none have so far been repainted in 'Railfreight' colours. No 56.097 stands outside Doncaster paint shop, illustrated from the No 1 end.   Colin J. Marsden

Below:
During the summer of 1980 locomotives Nos 56.073/074 were released from BREL Doncaster fitted with a remote control system for use in certain colliery lines in the Yorkshire area, enabling the locomotives to be controlled from a central point whilst operating in the power station complex. The locomotives were given yellow roof mounted beacons which flashed when the system was in use. No 56.074, with roof mounted light, arrives at Eggborough Power Station with a heavy MGR train. Colin J. Marsden

Above:
Naming of selected members of the Class 56 fleet commenced during June 1981 when some WR locomotives received corporate style plates. Further namings followed in 1982 including two ER locomotives named after industrial users of the class, No 56.074 Kellingley Colliery *departs from Doncaster with a northbound MGR train during the summer of 1982. It is understood that several further Class 56 namings will take place in the future.* Colin J. Marsden

Below:
With the object of reducing construction and maintenance costs, when No 56.042 was built it was fitted with a new design of bogie, designated CP1. After completion the locomotive operated a number of tests under the control of the Research Centre at Derby, prior to taking up normal duties and allocation to TO depot. It is a direct descendant from these bogies that the CP3, now fitted under Class 58 locomotives, has been developed. No 56.042 stands in the works yard at Doncaster during 1979.
Derek Porter

Class 58

Number series: 58.001-58.035
Built by: BREL Doncaster
Introduced: From 1982
Type: Co-Co
Weight in running order: 130 tonnes
Height: 12ft 10in (3.91m)
Width: 8ft 10½in (2.70m)
Length: 62ft 9½in (19.13m)
Min curve negotiable: 4 chains (80.00m)
Maximum speed: 80mph (129km/h)
Wheelbase: 48ft 9in (14.85m)
Bogie wheelbase: 13ft 8½in (4.18m)
Bogie pivot centres: 35ft 5½in (10.80m)
Wheel diameter — driving: 3ft 8in (1.12m)
Brake type: Air
Sanding equipment: Electro pneumatic
Route availability: 7

Coupling restriction: Red Diamond
Brake force: 75 tonnes (738kN)
Engine type: Ruston Paxman 12RK3ACT
HP: 3,300hp (2,460kW)
Tractive effort: 60,000lb (267kN)
Cylinder bore: 10in (0.25m)
Cylinder stroke: 12in (0.30m)
Main alternator type: Brush BA1101B
Aux alternator type: Brush BAA602B
Traction motor type: Brush TM73-62
Gear ratio: 63:16
Fuel tank capacity: 985gal (4,480lit)
Cooling water capacity: 264gal (1,200lit)
Lub oil capacity: 110gal (416lit)
Region of allocation: Midland
Works responsible for classified overhauls: Doncaster

Below:
The cost of design and building the Class 56 locomotives became prohibitively expensive quite early during the build, mainly due to the methods and style of construction, so during 1977 plans were drawn up for the next generation of heavy freight locomotive, the Class 58. This illustration gives the comparison of the two purpose built freight locomotives side by side outside Doncaster Works paint shop. The Class 56 is of monocoque construction, while Class 58 is modular. Derek Porter

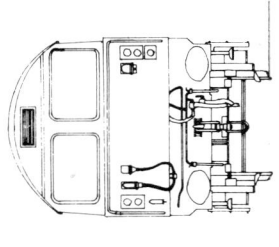

No. 2 END

No. 1 END

Above:
This is the latest BR designed locomotive. They are of modular construction, each major component being fitted to a rigid frame. No significant detail differences exist amongst the few locomotives in traffic. Both body sides are of identical layout.

Above:
Front end detail of Class 58: 1. Engine control air pipe, 2. Main reservoir pipe, 3. Brake pipe, 4. Multiple-unit (Red Diamond) control jumper cable, 5. Multiple-unit (Red Diamond) control jumper socket, 6. Red rear indicator light, 7. White frontal marker light, 8. Fixed beam headlight. Colin J. Marsden

Right:
The Class 58 design was completely new to BR engineering, being built up of sections, mounted on a rigid plate frame, enabling any module to be removed with ease. For example, if a locomotive was involved in a minor collision damaging a cab, just this part would be removed and replaced by a works stock item, enabling the locomotive to be out of revenue earning service for the minimum amount of time. With No 1 end nearest the camera, No 58.001 poses for the photographer outside its birthplace during December 1982. *Colin J. Marsden*

Centre right:
Orders have now been placed for 35 Class 58 heavy freight locomotives, all to be constructed at BREL Doncaster works. It is also envisaged that export orders may well follow once the locomotives are in traffic and can be inspected by other railway companies. The livery applied to the Class 58 is also new to BR with the main inset body section painted grey, with yellow cab sections and black window surrounds. The distinctive frame is painted signal red. Large numbers and BR logo are also applied. No 58.001 takes shape in the works E2 shop during mid-1982. *Colin J. Marsden*

Below right:
For the first time on a main line locomotive the Railfreight insignia is carried under the driver's assistant's cab side window, in white lettering on a red background. The Class 58 is mounted on a Co-Co wheel arrangement and the bogies are classified as CP3 and manufactured at BREL Crewe works. Each bogie has three Brush TM73-62 traction motors, one mounted on each wheel set. *Colin J. Marsden*

Class 253 and 254 Units

Power Cars
Number series: 43002-43198
Built by: BREL Crewe Works
Introduced: 1976-1982
Type: Bo-Bo
Weight in running order: 70 tonnes
Height: 12ft 9in (3.88m)
Width: 8ft 11in (2.71m)
Length: 58ft 5in (17.80m)
Maximum speed: 125mph (201km/h)
Wheelbase: 42ft 3in (12.87m)
Bogie wheelbase: 8ft 6in (2.59m)
Bogie pivot centres: 33ft 9in (10.28m)

Wheel diameter (new): 3ft 4in (1.01m)
Brake type: Air
Engine type: Paxman Valenta 12RP200L
HP: 2,250hp (1,676kW)
Control equipment: 4×Brush TMH68-46 (43002-123/153-198) 4×GEC G417A2 (43124-43152)
Tractive effort: 17,980lb (80kN)
Fuel tank capacity: 1,000gal (4,546lit)
Route availability: 6
Operating range: 1,400 miles (2,253km)

Note: Although not officially classified as locomotives, High Speed Trains (IC125s) have been included in this volume of *Motive Power Recognition* as considerable interest has been aroused by their power cars and, after all, each power car is an individual locomotive, capable of movement by itself.

Below:
The IC125 train sets are now used on four regions with only the Southern not having diagrammed services over its tracks. Various formations exist depending on the intended route for the unit. WR Class 253 set No 253.026 passes the site of the long closed Box station with a Bristol-Paddington express during the summer of 1980.
Colin J. Marsden

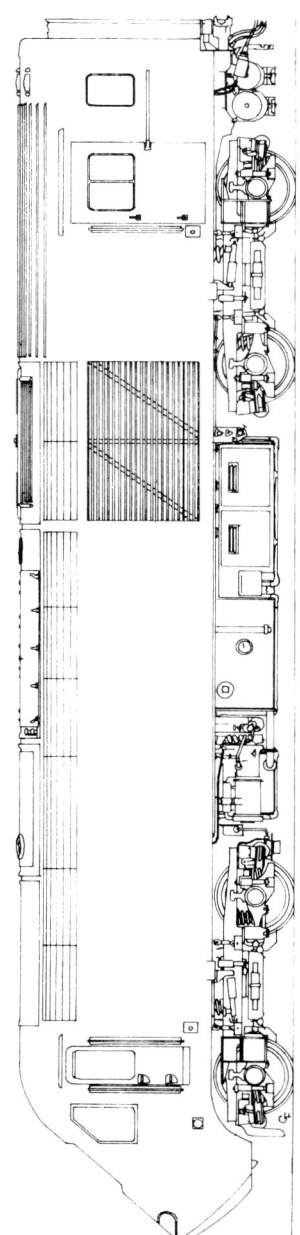
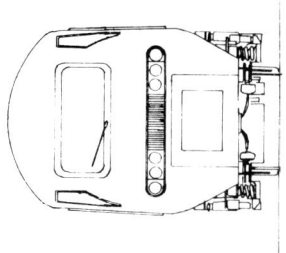

Above:
Two types of IC125 power car are in existence — DM (Driving Motor) and DMB (Driving Motor Brake). This drawing is of a DMB in the number range 43003-43152. Both sides of the car are identical. On DM cars, the window to the rear of the guard's door is omitted.

Above:
Two types of motor car have been constructed for IC125 operation: DMB — Driving Motor Brake and DM — Driving Motor. DMBs contain a guard's office but DMs do not, thus the single window at the far end after the luggage van door is omitted on DM vehicles. No 1 end of an IC125 power car is the driving end, and No 2 the luggage van end. Battery boxes are placed between the bogies, with fuel tank, compressor and brake equipment. A Class 253 DMB is illustrated here. Colin J. Marsden

Below:
This rear three-quarter view shows a DM — Driving Motor car, not provided with a guard's office. DM power cars are numbered 43153-198. The livery applied to the IC125 power cars is yellow/blue at the No 1 end which changes mid-way to standard InterCity colours. All IC125 power cars carry the legend 'InterCity 125' on their body sides. Colin J. Marsden

Above:
When the IC125 train system was developed it was foreseen that problems could arise if a set failed, as no buffing gear was provided and assistance in the conventional way could not be given. However a decision was made to fix all DM/DMB vehicles with hidden air pipes and draw hook under the nose end valance, with a separate coupling arm housed in the power car. When assistance is necessary the front valance is lifted, air pipes drawn out and coupling arm attached. This is being carried out here at Exeter where Class 47 No 47.123 is waiting to be attached. Any locomotive can be used to haul an IC125 as long as it is fitted with train air brake equipment. Dinky Talbot

Below:
Various standard formations of IC125 sets exist. WR internal sets are formed of a DM/DMB at each end with a TGS, TS, TS, TS, TRSB/TRUB, TF, TF between. These units are allocated to Old Oak Common, Bristol St Philips Marsh and Laira (Plymouth), but operate on all WR internal services. Units began emerging from Derby works in revised colours from mid-1983. Set No 253.030 passes Castle Cary. Colin J. Marsden

Above:
Class 253 units used to operate the NE/SW route are formed with an additional TS vehicle, due to the low number of first class patrons on the route. The formation of units is DM, TGS, TS, TS, TS, TS, TRSB, TF, DM, with second class accommodation normally at NE end of the formation. A NE/SW set climbs away from Totnes and heads towards Dainton with a Newcastle bound service. Colin J. Marsden

Note: From October 1982 some Class 253 sets were allocated to the ER for use on the St Pancras-Derby/Sheffield/Nottingham services; these are standard Class 253 formations.

Note: There are three usual formations for Class 254 sets, either formed with one or two refreshment vehicles, or an additional TS. Class 254 power cars are not officially allocated to any specific formation but classified as loose power cars and used as required. However for reporting purposes set numbers are retained but not applied, and only refer to the trailer vehicles.
Sets Nos 254.001-011 are formed TF, TF, TRUK, TRSB, TS, TS, TS, TGS.
Sets Nos 254.012-020 are formed TF, TF, TRUB, TS, TS, TS, TGS.
Sets Nos 254.021-037 are formed TF, TF, TRUB, TS, TS, TS, TS, TGS.
Sets Nos 254.038-043 are formed TF, TF, TRUB, TS, TS, TS, TGS.

Below:
All main line services on the ER are operated by IC125 formations and allocated to Bounds Green (BN), Neville Hill (NL), Heaton (HT) and Craigentinny (EC). One of the sets in the range 254.021-037 is illustrated here with the two TF vehicles at the London end of the formation which is normal operating practice. The unit is seen near Selby on 9 September 1981. Colin J. Marsden

Right:
Over the years it has become quite common during summer months to find misformed IC125 sets operating on the ECML, usually with additional TS vehicles in the formations. Here we see set 254.011 still sporting a number and formed TF, TF, TRSB, TS, TS, TS, TS, TGS, the additional TS taking the place of the TRUK. The set passes Rossington, south of Doncaster, during 1982.   Colin J. Marsden

Centre right:
If IC125 DM/DMB cars are required to operate on their own they are normally coupled to a match wagon (from the departmental fleet). DM No 43155 heads south on the outskirts of York coupled to a IC125 barrier coach which was formerly a Mk 1 BSK. These match vehicles can also be used to couple locomotives to the luggage ends of DM/DMB cars as one end of the barrier coach has conventional draw gear whilst the other has IC125 internal couplings.   John Tuffs

Below right:
Several recent modifications have been made to the IC125 fleet. Some DMB vehicles (in particular those operating the LMR service) have their car number painted on the nose end just above the horn grille, whilst some Class 254 cars have appeared in traffic with a black painted cab roof to try to eliminate the dirt effect of exhaust blow-down on the previously yellow paintwork. The most recent modification has been the naming of some ER DMB cars. DMB No 43107 with number painted on the nose end stands at Leicester.   Brian Morrison

Class 73

Number series: 73.001-73.006, 73.101-73.142*
Former number: E6001-E6049
Built by: BR Eastleigh/English Electric, Vulcan Foundry*
Introduced: 1962, 1967-68*
Type: Bo-Bo
Weight in running order: 75 tonnes, 76tonnes*
Height: 12ft 6⅛in (3.81m)
Width: 8ft 8in (2.64m)
Length: Buffer Extended 55ft 8in (16.96m)
Buffer Retracted 52ft 6in (16.00m)
Min curve negotiable: 4 chains (80.46m)
Maximum speed: 80mph (129km/h), 90mph* (145km/h)
Wheelbase: 40ft 9in (12.42m)
Bogie pivot centres: 32ft 0in (11.27m)
Wheel diameter: 3ft 4in (1.01m)
Brake type: Dual, EP
Sanding equipment: Pneumatic
Route availability: 6

Brake force: 31 tonnes
Diesel engine type: English Electric 4SRKT
HP: 1,600hp (1,192kW) Electric 600hp (447kW) Diesel
Tractive effort maximum: Diesel 34,100lb (152kN), 36,000lb* (160kN) Electric 42,000lb (187kN), 40,000lb* (179kN)
Main generator type: English Electric 824/3D
Aux generator type: English Electric 908/3C
Traction motor type: English Electric 542A, 546/1B*
Gear ratio: 62:17
Coupling restriction: Blue Star/and Electric within class
Normal supply voltage: 750v DC/or auxiliary diesel
ETH index: 66 (electric power only)
Region of allocation: Southern
Works responsible for classified overhauls: Eastleigh

Below:
One of the most versatile fleets of locomotives to be built are the SR Class 73 electro-diesel locomotives, able to operate either from the 660-750v DC third rail pick-up or from their own 600hp diesel engine. There are two types of Class 73 — 73/0 and 73/1. Only six '73/0s' were built by BR in 1962, but after successful trials a further fleet of 43 '73/1' was ordered from English Electric during 1966/7. Detail differences do exist. '73/1' No 73.142 Broadlands is seen from No 2 end at Stewarts Lane.*
Colin J. Marsden

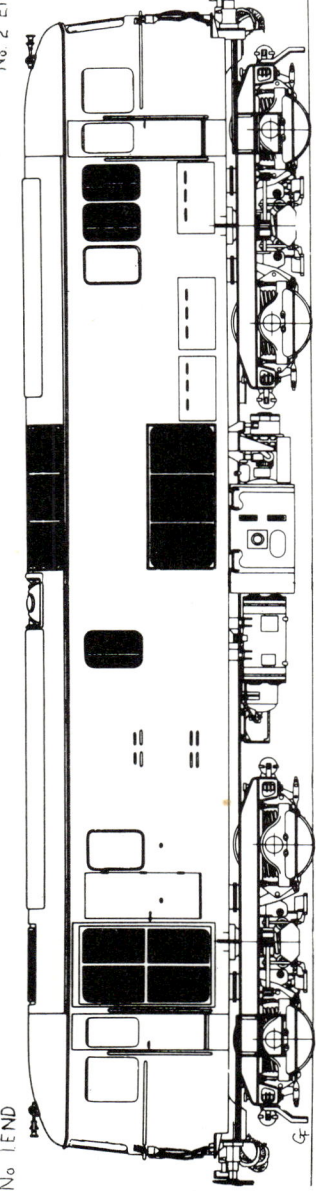

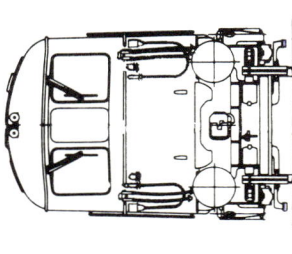

Above:
Two types of Class 73 are in service. Class 73/0, formed of six locomotives
Nos 73.001-006 are the prototypes built by BR at Eastleigh during the early 1960s;
Class 73/1 is currently made up of 41 members in the number range 73.101-142. This
drawing is of the original Class 73/0 locomotive. Class 73/1 have a revised layout and
reference to the illustrations is advised to establish detail differences.

Above:
Front end details of Class 73/0 (left) and Class 73/1 (right). The main recognition difference between the two types is the additional jumper cable under the driver's window, and socket under the driver's assistant's window. 1. Engine control air pipe, 2. Main reservoir pipe, 3. Vacuum pipe, 4. Air brake pipe, 5. Electric train heating jumper socket, 6. Electric train heating jumper cable, 7. Rubbing plate, 8. Buckeye coupling, 9. Waist height dual brake pipe/main reservoir isolating cock, 10. Waist height emu/loco control jumper cable, 11. Waist height emu/loco control jumper socket, 12. Additional waist height control jumper cable '73/0' only, 13. Additional waist height control jumper cable socket '73/0' only, 14. Emergency screw coupling (stowed in engine room when not in use). Brian Morrison/Colin J. Marsden

Below:
The first six Class 73 locomotives forming sub-section '0' were built by BR at Eastleigh works during 1962 and differ from the main production batch classified 73/1 in a number of ways — additional jumper cables on the nose end, bogie design, underframe equipment design and the number of side grilles/windows. When observed from No 2 end a Class 73/0 has two louvres and a window, whereas on a Class 73/1 only grilles are provided. No 73.004 is illustrated here; a fuel tank and MG set are between the bogies. Brian Cresswell

Above:
Class 73/1 viewed from No 1 end which, in common with all diesel locomotives, houses the radiator and coolant equipment. The door behind the radiator grille gives access to the diesel power unit when under maintenance. All Class 73s are allocated to Stewarts Lane depot from where they operate to all points on SR. No 73.107 is photographed standing outside the fuelling shed at its home depot. Colin J. Marsden
Note: *From late 1983 a start was made on painting the class in revised livery, similar to that carried on Class 50s.*

Below:
During 1984 three members of the Class 73 fleet carry names, No 73.101 Brighton Evening Argus, *No 73.121* Croydon 1883-1983, *No 73.129* City of Winchester, *and probably the most famous SR locomotive ever built No 73.142* Broadlands *which has been involved in numerous Royal events including the Royal Wedding, the funeral train for Lord Mountbatten of Burma, whose home the locomotive is named after, and the Papal visit. The distinctive nameplate of No 73.142 is shown here with the two heraldic crests below.* Colin J. Marsden

Class 81

Number series: 81.001-81.022
Former number: E3001-E3023,
E3096-E3097
Built by: Birmingham Railway Carriage
& Wagon Co
Introduced: 1959-1960
Type: Bo-Bo
Weight in running order: 79 tonnes
Height — pan down: 12ft 4¼in (3.76m)
Width: 8ft 8½in (2.65m)
Length: 56ft 6in (17.22m)
Min curve negotiable: 4 chains
(80.46m)
Maximum speed: 100mph (151km/h)
Wheelbase: 42ft 3in (12.87m)
Bogie pivot centres: 31ft 6in (9.60m)

Wheel diameter: 4ft 0in (1.21m)
Brake type: Dual
Heating type: Electric — Index 66
Route availability: 6
Brake force: 40 tonnes
HP maximum: 3,200hp (2,384kW)
Tractive effort maximum: 50,000lb
(222kN)
Traction motor type: AEI 189
Gear ratio: 29:76
Pantograph type: Stone-Faiveley
Rectifier type; Mercury Arc
Nominal supply voltage: 25kV AC
Region of allocation: Scottish
**Works responsible for classified
overhauls:** Crewe

Below:
The pioneer fleet of LMR 25kV electric locomotives emerged from Birmingham Railway Carriage & Wagon Company works during 1959. When constructed the locomotives initially carried two pantographs, but one was subsequently removed. Under the BR classification system these original locomotives became Class 81 and are still in regular operation on the 25kV sections of LMR and ScR and allocated to Glasgow Shields Road traction depot. The two sides of the Class 81 are totally different, one having nine ventilator grilles mid-way up the body side and the other having four windows. No 81.001, the pioneer locomotive, is seen at Euston. Steve Montgomery

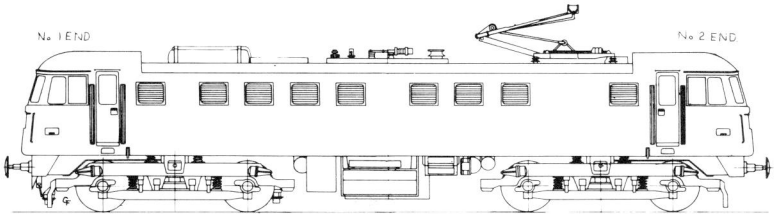

Above:
This drawing is representative of the majority of this class. The window and ventilation arrangement on the opposite side of the body is different.

Below:
The recognition of No 1 end on the overhead electric locomotive fleet is comparatively easy if it is remembered that the power collection pantograph is always positioned at No 2 end. Underslung equipment between the bogies consists of weak field resistances, rectifiers, battery box, exhauster/compressor and smoothing chokes. With No 1 end nearest to the camera No 81.007 stands at Euston during 1981.
Colin J. Marsden

Class 82

Number series: 82.001-82.008
Former number: E3046-E3055
Built by: Beyer Peacock Ltd, Gorton
Introduced: 1960-61
Type: Bo-Bo
Weight in running order: 78ton 4cwt (78.2 tonnes)
Height — pan down: 12ft 4¼in (3.76m)
Width: 8ft 9in (2.66m)
Length: 56ft 0in (17.06m)
Minimum curve negotiable: 4 chains (80.46m)
Maximum speed: 100mph (161km/h)
Wheelbase: 40ft 9in (12.42m)
Bogie pivot centres: 30ft 9in (9.37m)
Wheel diameter: 4ft 0in (1.21m)

Brake type: Dual
Heating type: Electric — Index 66
Route availability: 6
Brake force: 38 tonnes
HP Maximum: 3,320hp (2,473kW)
Tractive effort maximum: 50,000lb (222kN)
Traction motor type: AEI 189Z
Gear ratio: 29:76
Pantograph type: Stone Faiveley/AEI
Rectifier type: Mercury Arc
Nominal supply voltage: 25kV AC
Region of allocation: Midland
Works responsible for classified overhauls: Crewe
Class scheduled for early withdrawal

Below:
Of the five pioneer classes of 25kV electric locomotives ordered, each was built by a different main manufacturer, thus evaluating different equipment. The second fleet classified as Class 82 were constructed by Beyer Peacock of Gorton, Manchester. The basic design of the body is the same as for Class 81 but grilles and windows are in different positions. Originally locomotives had four position headcodes but these were later blanked out with just two white central discs showing, however in recent years the panels have been plated over and two sealed beam headlights fitted. No 82.001 passes Nuneaton with an up special during 1982.   Colin J. Marsden

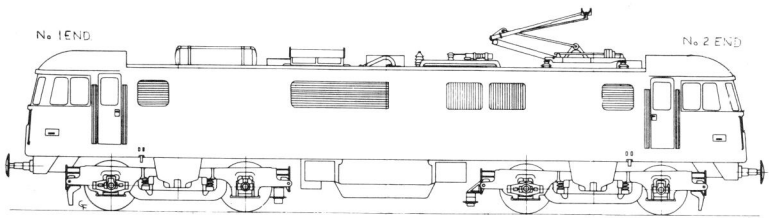

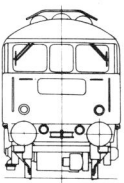

Above:
This drawing is representative of the majority of this class. The window and ventilation arrangement on the opposite side of the body is different.

Below:
Class 82 viewed from No 2 end showing the grille side of the body with five separate grille blocks, each giving ventilation to internal electrical equipment. Batteries, compressor, weak field resistances and auxiliary transformer are placed between the bogies. No 82.004 is illustrated here in a line of Class 82 and 83 locomotives stored at Longsight, Manchester. Steve Turner

Note: All members of Class 82 were stored at the beginning of 1983 but not all in a serviceable condition. At present it is uncertain what the future holds for these locomotives.

Class 83

Number series: 83.001-83.015
Former number: E3024-E3035, E3098-E3100
Built by: English Electric Company, Vulcan Foundry
Introduced: 1960-1961
Type: Bo-Bo
Weight in running order: 73 tonnes
Height — pan down: 12ft 4¼in (3.76m)
Width: 8ft 8½in (2.65m)
Length: 57ft 6in (17.52m)
Minimum curve negotiable: 4 chains (80.46m)
Maximum speed: 100mph (161km/h)
Wheelbase: 40ft 0in (12.19m)
Bogie pivot centres: 30ft 0in (9.14m)
Wheel diameter: 4ft 0in (1.21m)

Brake type: Dual
Heating type: Electric — Index 66
Route availability: 6
Brake force: 38 tonnes
HP Maximum: 2,950hp (1,900kW)
Tractive effort maximum: 38,000lb (169kN)
Traction motor type: English Electric 535A
Gear ratio: 25:76
Pantograph type: Stone Faiveley
Rectifier type: Mercury Arc
Nominal supply voltage: 25kV AC
Region of allocation: Midland
Works responsible for classified overhauls: Crewe
Class scheduled for early withdrawal

Below:
Fifteen locomotives were built by English Electric at their Vulcan Foundry works in Newton-le-Willows during 1960 and under BR numerical classification these became Class 83. The same basic external design as previous 25kV classes was followed with minor differences. Again body details differ with one side having four rectangular air louvres but the other having two windows and one air louvre; originally three windows were fitted. No 83.011 is viewed from No 2 end prior to the abolition of the four character headcode system in 1975, at AN depot. Barry Nicolle

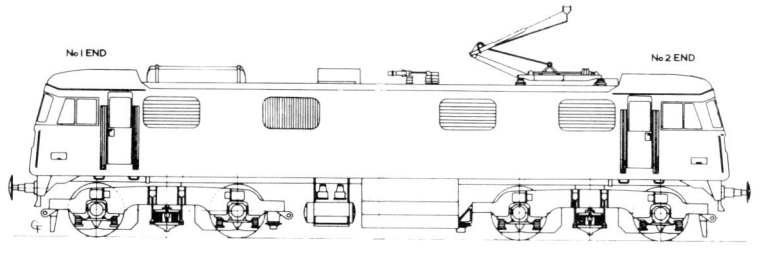

Above:
This drawing is representative of the majority of this class. The window and ventilation arrangement on the opposite side of the body is different.

Below:
When built the Class 83 fleet, in common with other pioneer electric classes, were fitted with vacuum braking and two pantographs but the one at No 1 end was removed soon after entering regular service. Dual braking was fitted when the fleet was refurbished at BREL Doncaster during the early 1970s and at the same time three large main reservoir tanks were placed on the roof at No 1 end. All Class 83s are allocated to Longsight depot, Manchester. No 83.015 is seen at Euston with empty stock bound for the nearby carriage sidings. Barry Edwards

Note: All members of Class 83 were stored at the beginning of 1983 but not all in serviceable condition. At present it is uncertain what the future holds for these locomotives.

Class 85

Number series: 85.001-85.040
Former number: E3056-E3095
Built by: BR Doncaster
Introduced: 1961-1962
Type: Bo-Bo
Weight in running order: 80 tonnes
Height — pan down: 12ft 4¼in (3.76m)
Width: 8ft 8¾in (2.66m)
Length: 56ft 5in (17.19m)
Minimum curve negotiable: 6 chains (120.70m)
Maximum speed: 100mph (161km/h)
Wheelbase: 42ft 3in (12.87m)
Bogie pivot centres: 31ft 6in (9.60m)
Wheel diameter: 4ft 0in (1.21m)
Brake type: Dual (Rheostatic)
Heating type: Electric — Index 66
Route availability: 6
Brake force: 41 tonnes
HP: 3,200hp (2,384kW)
Tractive effort maximum: 50,000lb (222kN)

Traction motor type: AEI 189
Gear ratio: 29:76
Pantograph type: Stone Faiveley
Rectifier type: Germanium
Nominal supply voltage: 25kV DC
Region of allocation: Midland
Works responsible for classified overhauls: Crewe

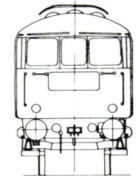

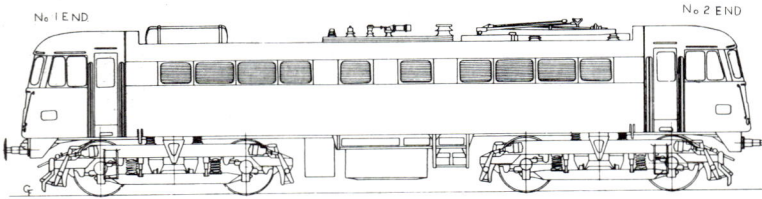

Above:
This drawing is representative of the majority of this class. The window and ventilation arrangement on the opposite side of the body is different.

Right:
The first 25kV locomotives to be constructed by BR was a fleet of 40 AL5 later Class 85 units, being built from 1961 by the BR workshops at Doncaster. The body followed previous designs but with detail differences and the body sides differing. In this view of No 85.012 we see the grilled side where the majority of electrical equipment is carried. This picture is taken from No 1 end.   Colin J. Marsden

Right:
Front end layout for Class 85 locomotive; this layout is also applicable to Classes 81-83, although some equipment may differ slightly in position.
1. Vacuum pipe, 2. Draw hook, with shackle below, 3. Air brake pipe, 4. Main reservoir pipe, 5. Electric train heating jumper socket, 6. Electric train heating jumper cable, 7. Red rear marker light, 8. Air warning horns. The former four position headcode on the majority of locomotives has now been plated over.
Colin J. Marsden

Below:
Class 85 viewed from No 2 end, showing the window side of the locomotive. It is quite surprising to see that the majority of older electric locomotive classes still retain their aluminium BR logo, which is centrally applied. The equipment visible between the bogies on the Class 85 consists of smoothing chokes which are forced air cooled by a centrally mounted fan.
Steve Montgomery

Class 86

Number series: 86.001-10/30-39, 86.101-103, 86.204-261, 86.311-329
Former number: E3101-E3200
Built by: BR Doncaster, English Electric Vulcan Foundry
Introduced: 1965-66
Type: Bo-Bo
Weight in running order: 86 tonnes (86/2), 83 tonnes (86/0, 86/3), 87 tonnes (86/1)
Height — pan down: 13ft 0⁹/₁₆in (7.93m)
Width: 8ft 8¼in (2.64m)
Length: 58ft 6in (17.83m)
Minimum curve negotiable: 6 chains (120.70m)
Maximum speed: 100mph (161km/h)
Wheelbase: 43ft 6in (13.25m)
Bogie pivot centres: 32ft 9in (9.98m)
Wheel diameter: 3ft 9in (1.14m)
Brake type: Dual/rheostatic
Heating type: Electric — Index 66

Route availability: 6
Brake force: 40 tonnes
HP Maximum: 5,900hp (4,400kW) (86/0, 86/3), 5,000hp (3,729kW) (86/1), 6,100hp (4,544kW) (86/2)
Tractive effort maximum: 58,000lb (258kN) (86/0, 86/1, 86/3), 46,500lb† (207kN) (86/2)
Traction motor type: AEI 282AZ (86/0, 86/3) GEC G412AZ (86/1) AEI 282BZ (86/2)
Gear ratio: 22:65 (86/10, 86/2, 86/3) 32:73 (86/1)
Pantograph type: Stone Faiveley/AEI
Rectifier type: Silicon semi Conductor
Nominal supply voltage: 25kV AC
Region of allocation: Midland
Works responsible for classified overhauls: Crewe

Below:
By far the largest fleet of AC electric locomotives is the 100 members of Class 86, divided into four sub-classes, 86/0-86/3. All are allocated to Willesden depot in London and can be seen operating on express passenger and freight services throughout the LMR/ScR 25kV electrified network. Class 86/2 No 86.254 William Webb Ellis *passes Grayrigg with the 08.10 Birmingham-Glasgow of 9 February 1983.* Colin J. Marsden

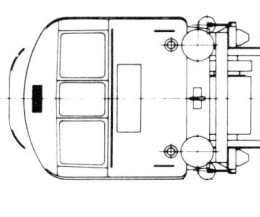

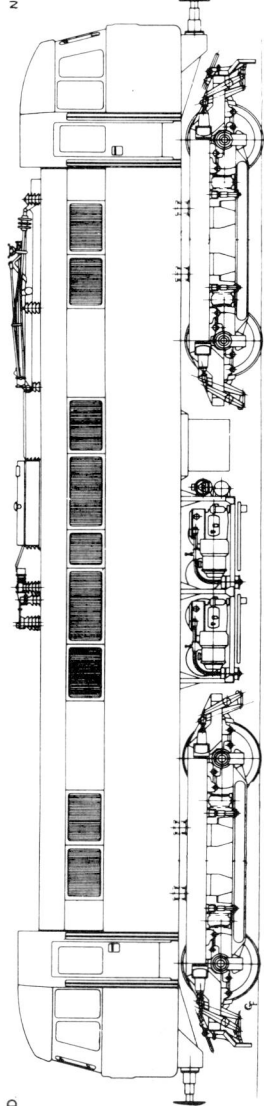

Above:
Several detail differences exist within the Class 86 fleet, mainly involving bogie and underframe mounted equipment. This drawing represents most members of the Class 86/0 fleet. For detail differences within the class, reference should be made to the illustrations.

Left:
Front end detail of Class 86 locomotive. Note: Not all locomotives have the quartz headlight (No 7), and all locomotives now have a plated route indicator fitted with two sealed beam headlights.
1. Electric train heating jumper socket, 2. Vacuum pipe, 3. Air brake pipe, 4. Main reservoir pipe, 5. Electric train heating jumper cable, 6. Red rear indicator lights, 7. Quartz headlight.
British Railways

Below:
Class 86/0: Of the original 100 members of Class 86 only 20 remain in their original form; these are now classified as Class 86/0. This sub-class, although fitted with electric train supply facilities is intended for freight train operation and restricted to 80mph. Recognition between Class 86/0 and 86/1 or 86/2 is easy, as no secondary body mounted springs are fitted on Class 86/0. A number of Class 86/0s are fitted for multiple operation. Two Class 86/0s Nos 86.038/004 descend Shap Bank with an up steel train.
Colin J. Marsden

Above:
Class 86/2: 61 members of the original 100 AL6, later Class 86 locomotives, were rebuilt to express passenger standards at BREL Crewe works from 1972 and classified '86/2'. The modification work included fitting flexicoil suspension and resilient wheels. This view of No 86.226 Mail *is taken from No 1 end looking at the side of the locomotive which houses two banks of two air louvres and two windows. The flexicoil suspension and associated dampers can clearly be observed in this illustration.*
Colin J. Marsden

Below:
Class 86/3: 19 members of the 80mph Class 86/0 fleet were modified to 86/3 during the early 1980s and fitted with SAB resilient wheels permitting the maximum speed to be increased to 100mph, thus improving the operating potential of these locomotives. Many of the sub-class are fitted with multiple control equipment identifiable by the jumper and socket on the nose end. No 86.313 passes Castlethorpe.
Michael Collins

Above:
To assist track staff in the sighting of approaching fast trains a number of alternative headlight designs have been tested on various locomotives, and one of the latest seen on a Class 86 is shown here. It is a single fixed beam spotlight, similar to that of a motor car spotlight, centrally mounted on the nose end under the former route indicator panel. No 86.225 Hardwicke *sporting this modification passes Stafford.*
Michael Collins

Below:
In association with the 1980 'Rocket 150 Celebrations' to mark the 150th anniversary of the Liverpool & Manchester Railway, two Class 86/2 locomotives Nos 86.214/235 were painted in revised livery with large numerals and a Liverpool-Manchester Railway embellishment on the side. No 86.235 Novelty *is seen here at Euston with the grilled bodyside nearest to the camera.* Steven Montgomery

Top:
The Class 86/1 and 86/2 express passenger/freight locomotives were selected to be one of the classes to carry corporate style nameplates during the late 1970s. Most members have been allocated names and it is likely that the Class 86/3 fleet will also be named in the future. This slightly non-standard plate Josiah Wedgwood *is applied to No 86.236.* Colin J. Marsden

Above:
Standard corporate identity style plate as affixed to No 86.257 Snowdon.
Barry Edwards

Below:
To evaluate technical equipment scheduled for installation in the projected Class 87 locomotives, three Class 86s were rebuilt with modified apparatus. The main difference was the fitting of Class 87 style bogies, traction equipment and modified underframe modules; Quartz fixed beam headlights were also fitted. This illustration shows the number, area and identification plate of No 86.102, this locomotive was orginally numbered 86.202. Colin J. Marsden

Class 87

Number series: 87.001-87.035, *87.101
Built by: BREL Crewe
Introduced: 1973-1977
Type: Bo-Bo
Weight in running order: 81ton 19cwt (82 tonnes) 77ton 17cwt* (77.9 tonnes)
Height — pan down: 13ft 1¼in (3.99m)
Width: 8ft 8¼in (2.64m)
Length: 58ft 6in (17.83m)
Minimum curve negotiable: 6 chains (120.70m)
Maximum speed: 100mph (161km/h)
Wheelbase: 43ft 6⅛in (13.25m)
Bogie pivot centres: 32ft 9in (9.98m)
Wheel diameter: 3ft 9½in (1.15m)

Brake type: Air (Rheostatic)
Heating type: Electric — Index 66
Route availability: 6
Brake force: 40 tonnes
HP: 5,000hp (3,725kW), 4,850hp* (3,613kW)
Tractive effort maximum: 58,000lb (258kN)
Traction motor type: GEC G412AZ, G412BZ*
Gear ratio: 32:73
Pantograph type: GEC
Rectifier type: Silicon semi conductor
Nominal supply voltage: 25kV AC
Region of allocation: Midland
Works responsible for classified overhauls: Crewe

Below:
The newest 25kV electric class in service are the 36 members of Class 87/0 and 87/1, introduced for use on the Anglo Scottish services from 1973. All conform to the same basic layout as previous AC classes with the exception of only two front windows instead of three. No 87.014 Knight of the Thistle *passes Nuneaton with a Euston bound express during the spring of 1983.* Colin J. Marsden

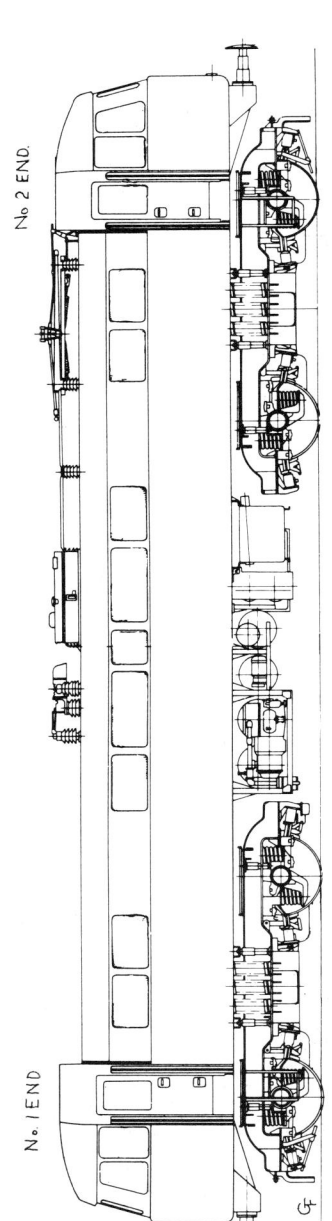

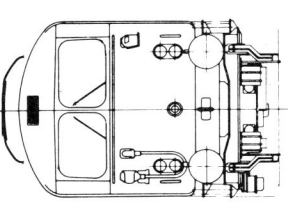

No 2 END.

No. 1 END

Above:
This drawing is representative of the majority of the class, fitted with a cross arm pantograph. Window and ventilation arrangements differ on either side of the body.

Left:
*Class 87 front end layout:
1. Electric train heat jumper
socket, 2. Electric train heat
jumper cable, 3. Air brake pipe,
4. Main reservoir pipe,
5. Multiple-unit control jumper
cable, 6. Multiple-unit control
jumper socket, 7. Red rear
indicator light, 8. White frontal
marker light, 9. Fixed beam
headlight.* Colin J. Marsden

Below:
*The two sides of the Class 87
fleet differ with one side having
two banks of two grilles and two
mid-position windows, whilst the
other side has a near complete
line of ventilation grilles by the
main electrical equipment.
No 87.016* Sir Francis Drake *is
viewed from No 2 end
(pantograph end).*
Colin J. Marsden

Top right:
Class 87 No 87.024 Lord of the
Isles *viewed from No 2 end,
showing the opposite side (grille
side) to the previous plate. All
Class 87s are allocated to
Willesden (WN) and used over the
complete 25kV network of the
LMR/ScR lines, both on passenger
and freight duties.*
Colin J. Marsden

Centre right:
A recent modification to No 87.004 Britannia *is an additional train communication jumper, mounted on the locomotive's nose end. This fitment is usually used when hauling the Royal Train. This additional jumper is clearly visible in this view of No 87.004 passing Watford Junction with the 10.19 Blackpool-Euston on 21 May 1983.* Michael Collins

Below:
The final production Class 87, originally allocated No 87.036, was selected for test purposes and fitted with GEC Thyristor control equipment. After this modification the locomotive became non-standard and therefore classified '87/1', numbered 87.101, and is now named Stephenson. *The external appearance is the same as the Class 87/0 fleet but internal equipment has altered considerably. The purpose of this modification was to evaluate the effect of Thyristor control on tractive effort performance and to have available a full sized test bed for further development in the Thyristor field.* Brian Morrison

Departmental Locomotives
Class 97

Departmental Number	Name	Former No	Use	Location
97.201	*Experiment*	RDB968007	Trial locomotive	Derby Technical Centre
97.202	—	25.131	Test locomotive	Toton
97.250	*ETHEL 1*	25.310	ETH generator	Eastfield
97.251	*ETHEL 2*	25.305	ETH generator	Eastfield
97.252	*ETHEL 3*	25.314	ETH generator	Eastfield
97.401	—	46.009	Test locomotive	Derby
97.402	—	46.023	Test locomotive	Toton
97.650	—	PWM 650	P/w locomotive	Swindon
97.651	—	PWM 651	P/w locomotive	Swindon (used at Radyr)
97.652	—	PWM 652	P/w locomotive	Taunton
97.653	—	PWM 653	P/w locomotive	Reading
97.654	—	PWM 654	P/w locomotive	Swindon
97.701	—	M61136	Battery locomotive	Birkenhead
97.702	—	M61139	Battery locomotive	Birkenhead
97.703	—	M61182	Battery locomotive	Cricklewood
97.704	—	M61184	Battery locomotive	Cricklewood
97.705	—	M61185	Battery locomotive	Cricklewood
97.706	—	M61189	Battery locomotive	Cricklewood
97.707	—	M61166	Battery locomotive	Glasgow Shields Road
97.708	—	M61173	Battery locomotive	Glasgow Shields Road
97.709	—	M61172	Battery locomotive	Hornsey (Stored)
97.710	—	M61175	Battery locomotive	Hornsey (Stored)
97.800	*Ivor*	08.600	Shed pilot	Slade Green
97.801	*Pluto*	08.267	Research loco	Derby Technical Centre
97.803	—	05.001	P/w locomotive	Ryde (IoW) (Stored)
97.804	—	06.003	S&T locomotive	Reading
P01	—	08.173	Shed pilot	Polmadie
D2991	—	—	Generator loco	Eastleigh
ADB968000	—	D8243	Generator loco	Bristol Carriage Sidings
ADB968021	—	84.009	Load bank	Cricklewood
ADB968022	—	84.003	Research loco	Derby Technical Centre
ADB975812	—	43.000	Research loco	Derby (Stored)
ADB975813	—	43.001	Research loco	Derby (Stored)

Bottom left:
The Railway Technical Centre at Derby houses the Research & Development Section, who operate a sizeable vehicle fleet mainly formed of coaching, NPCCS and wagon vehicles; however some locomotives are utilised by the Department. After withdrawal, Class 24 No 24.061 was taken over to provide motive power for test trains and was first renumbered RDB968007 and later 97,201 and named Experiment. *Current livery is red/blue with full yellow ends.* John Chalcraft

Above:
Ruston & Hornsby Ltd built five 165hp 0-6-0 shunting locomotives for the WR CCE Department in 1953 and were originally numbered in the Permanent Way Machine number series; renumbered into the Class 97 series during the late 1970s. The locomotives are allocated to RG, SW, Radyr and Taunton and can usually be found in permanent way yards or in action on weekend engineering sites. Some locomotives are painted in BR blue whilst others are in departmental yellow. No 97.652 is shown here, painted in BR blue. Barry Nicolle

Below:
The two former Class 41, later Class 252, prototype IC125 power cars were taken over by the Research Centre after withdrawal, mainly to provide traction power for test trains involved in the APT project and HST development. The two cars are currently stored at Derby works having completed their departmental use. The cars were renumbered ADB975812 and ADB975813 when in departmental use and are seen here providing traction/driving facilities for two APT power cars involved in brake tests, passing Warrington. Peter Spilsbury

Above:
A fleet of battery electric service locomotives, used in pairs, were rebuilt by BREL Doncaster during 1978/80 from redundant Class 501 EMU cars. The purpose of this conversion was to provide traction power for engineering trains involved in new electrification projects mainly in the Liverpool, Glasgow and London areas. During conversion all seating bays were removed as were most doors except two on each side; batteries were housed in the former seating areas. No 97.703 formerly M61182, stands outside Doncaster Works during January 1980.   Colin J. Marsden

Below:
The SR has a sizeable CM&EE workshop at Slade Green, near Dartford in Kent, which is responsible for repairs to SR locomotives, EMU and DMU stock. To assist in yard shunting manoeuvres a Departmental shunting locomotive is provided, No 97.800 Ivor, this was formerly Class 08, No 08.600. Livery applied is red/blue with yellow wasp ends.   Colin J. Marsden

Above:
The Isle of Wight railway network hosts one diesel locomotive amongst its otherwise EMU world. The locomotive, formerly Class 05 No 05.001, was transferred to Departmental stock during 1981 and numbered 97.803. It is used on ballast trains usually only during the winter months, being stabled for most of its life in sidings adjacent to Sandown station. No 97.803 is painted in standard shunting locomotive livery and is fitted with vacuum train brakes. This locomotive was withdrawn in the autumn of 1983. Colin J. Marsden

Below:
The Research & Development Section at Derby are the owners of one former Class 08, No 08.267. This locomotive is now numbered 97.801 and named Pluto, *being engaged in automatic train control development. The locomotive is still in rail blue livery and operates on test tracks.* BR

Above:
Following withdrawal of the Class 84 AC electric fleet, No 84.009 was transferred to the departmental fleet as a CM&EE mobile load bank for testing overhead power equipment. The locomotive is not self propelled. For most of the early 1980s this unit has operated from Cricklewood on the Bed-Pan electrification scheme. After conversion to a departmental vehicle No 84.009 was renumbered ADB968021. The vehicle was photographed at Cricklewood. Michael Collins

Below:
The Scottish Region has a small workshop at Polmadie on the outskirts of Glasgow, where repairs to shunting and main line diesel locomotives can be undertaken when it does not necessitate transfer to the main BREL works. Former Class 08 No 08.173 now numbered PO1 is used on depot pilot duties; this is a standard Class 08 locomotive and for technical detail please refer to the Class 08 section. The livery is standard rail blue with wasp ends. Tom Noble.

Above:
To pre-heat passenger stock, the ER converted four redundant Class 15 locomotives to non self-propelled generator vehicles; only one now remains, No ADB968000, currently in use at Bristol Bath Road carriage sidings for heating Mk III sleeping car stock. ADB968000 is seen here after repaint and repairs, at Colchester. Michael Collins

Below:
To enable ETH rolling stock to operate over northern sections of the Scottish Region — where ETH fitted locomotives are barred — three ETHEL (Electric Train Heat Ex-Locomotives) were introduced, being converted from redundant Class 25/3s. The units, with traction equipment isolated or removed, are coupled between the train locomotive and stock. ETHEL 1, No 97250 formerly Class 25/3 No 25.310 is shown here. Tom Noble.

Class 98

Number:	7	8	9
Built by:	GWR Swindon	GWR Swindon	Davis & Metcalfe
Introduced:	1923	1923	1902
Type:	2-6-2T	2-6-2T	2-6-2T
Weight in running order:	25 tons	25 tons	22 tons
Height:	9ft 0in	9ft 0in	9ft 0in
Width:	8ft 0in	8ft 0in	6ft 0in
Length:	21ft 10in	21ft 10in	21ft 10in
Wheelbase (coupled):	6ft 0in	6ft 0in	6ft 0in
Wheelbase (total):	16ft 10in	16ft 10in	16ft 10in
Coupled wheel diameter:	2ft 6in	2ft 6in	2ft 6in
Pony truck wheel diameter:	2ft 0in	2ft 0in	2ft 0in
Boiler pressure:	165lb/sq in	165lb/sq in	150lb/sq in
Coal capacity:	32cu ft	32cu ft	32cu ft
Water capacity:	520gal	520gal	650gal
Cylinders diameter × stroke:	$11\frac{1}{2}$in×17in	$11\frac{1}{2}$in×17in	11in×17in
Allocation:	Vale of Rheidol Railway	Vale of Rheidol Railway	Vale of Rheidol Railway
Works reponsible for classified overhaul:	Swindon	Swindon	Swindon

Below:
Vale of Rheidol locomotive No 9 Prince of Wales *built in 1902 by Davies & Metcalfe, is the oldest locomotive in use on a BR line. The locomotive is painted in yellow ochre livery, and photographed here arriving at Llanbadarn Halt with the 14.15 Aberystwyth-Devils Bridge on 26 June 1982. The Vale of Rheidol 1ft 11in gauge line operates the $11\frac{1}{2}$ miles from Aberystwyth to Devils Bridge from Easter to the end of October each year.* John Vaughan

Above:
No 8 Owain Glyndwr *was built in 1923 by the GWR and painted in BR blue with double arrow logo in recent years, however it is now in BR green livery with dart board style insignia. No 7 is painted in BR blue in this illustration.* Brian Morrison

Below:
This period illustration of No 7 Owain Glyndwr *taken at Aberystwyth in the summer of 1963, shows the locomotive painted in BR lined green livery with running number on the cab side and smokebox.* W. L. Underhay

Above:
No 8 Llewellyn *was also built by the GWR in 1923, and like Nos 7 and 9 also carried BR loco blue livery for many years up to 1981, when it was repainted in GWR green with round GWR crest on the cab side and running number at cab top height.* BR